Umberto Eco is Professor of Semiotics at Bologna University. He is the author of the novels *The Name of the Rose, Foucault's Pendulum, Baudolino and The Island of the Day Before*, as well as several collections of essays including *Semiotics and the Philosophy of Language, The Limits of Interpretation, Kant and the Platypus, Travels in Hyperreality, The Search for the Perfect Language, Serendipities* and *Six Walks in the Fictional Woods.*

Also by Umberto Eco

Kant and the Platypus
Semiotics and the Philosophy of Language
A Theory of Semiotics
Travels in Hyperreality
Misreadings
Faith in Fakes
The Name of the Rose
Reflections on The Name of the Rose
Foucault's Pendulum
The Island of the Day Before
Baudolino
Serendipities
Mouse or Rat?

Mouse or Rat?

Translation as Negotiation

UMBERTO ECO

PHOENIX

A PHOENIX PAPERBACK

First published in Great Britain in 2003
by Weidenfeld & Nicolson
This paperback edition published in 2004
by Phoenix,
an imprint of Orion Books Ltd,
Orion House, 5 Upper St Martin's Lane,
London WC2H 9EA

A CIP catalogue record for this book
is available from the British Library.

ISBN 0 75381 798 5

Printed and bound in Great Britain by
Clays Ltd St Ives plc

www.orionbooks.co.uk

Contents

Introduction

In October 1988 I delivered a series of three Goggio Lectures on translation at Toronto University.[1] At the same time, over a period of two years, I held seminars at the University of Bologna on the concept of intersemiotic translation, that is, the transformation of a novel into a film, or of a painting into a poem and so on.

In the course of those discussions I argued against the exaggeratedly indulgent idea of translation that charmed some of my students and colleagues. I therefore decided to examine more closely the idea of translation in the proper sense of the word, that is, the version from a text A in a verbal language Alpha into a text B in a verbal language Beta. Some of these reflections were presented at the Weidenfeld Lectures given at Oxford in 2002, and are published in this book in the form of essays.[2]

As I said when opening my Goggio Lectures, I frequently feel irritated when I read essays on the theory of translation that, even though brilliant and perceptive, do not provide enough examples. If they are not as rich in quotations as Steiner's *After Babel*, they are as bad as a book on dinosaurs that lacks any attempt to reconstruct the image of a dinosaur. I think that in addition to having made an intensive study of translations, of course, translation scholars should have had at least one of the following experiences during their life: translating, checking and editing translations, or being translated and working in close co-operation with their translators.

Active or passive experience in translation is not irrelevant for the formulation of theoretical reflections on the subject. In my Weidenfeld Lectures, therefore, my primary aim was to consider certain problems that I have tried to solve not as a translation theorist or as a semiotician interested in translation, but as an editor, a translator and a translated author. As an editor I worked for twenty years in a publishing house (and I still edit two series) and I had and still have to check many translations made by somebody else. As a translator I made only two translations, which took me many years of reflection and hard work; these were from the *Exercices de style* by Queneau[3] and Gérard de Nerval's *Sylvie*.[4] As an author I have almost always collaborated with my translators, and not only in the tongues I knew: I also succeeded in collaborating with translators in languages I did not know, for the simple reason that they were able to explain to me the kind of problem they were facing in their own language, asking for suggestions or for permission to change some details of the original text (it happened for instance with my Russian, Japanese, Hungarian and Dutch translators). My experience of collaboration started with my early essays and became more and more intense with my four novels.[5] Naturally, in reconsidering those experiences, I shall not avoid theoretical considerations, but I repeat that my lectures did not represent a systematic approach to translation but rather a series of reflections on my particular experiences.

It must be clear that my subject matter is what Jakobson called *translation proper* (that is, from one natural language into another). Thus I shall always use the term *translation* in its proper sense, and when speaking of other kinds of so-called 'translation' I shall put the term into inverted commas or I shall speak of intersemiotic translation or transmutation.

Irrespective of the fact that some philosophers or linguists have said that there are no rules for deciding whether one translation is better than another one, the everyday activity in a publishing house tells us that, at least in cases of blatant misunderstanding, it is easy to establish that a translation is wrong and deserves severe editing. Maybe it is only a question of common sense, but common sense must be respected.

In terms of common sense I ask you to imagine you have given a translator a printed manuscript in Italian (to be translated, let us say, into English), format A4, font Times Roman 12 point, 200 pages. If the translator brings you back, as an English equivalent of the source text, 400 pages in the same format, you are entitled to smell some form of misdemeanour. I believe one would be entitled to fire the translator before opening his or her product. If on the contrary we give a movie director the shortest novel ever written in the world, by Augusto Monterroso:

Cuando despertó, el dinosaurio todavia estaba allí.
(When he/she woke up, the dinosaur was still there.)

and the director brings us a tape two hours long, we do not have as yet any criterion to decide if the result is acceptable. We should first watch the tape in order to understand how the director has interpreted and adapted such an uncanny story through images.

Walt Disney 'translated' *Pinocchio* into a movie. One can say that Disney's idea of Pinocchio was different from the one transmitted by the early artists who illustrated Collodi's text, or that many elements of the story have been changed; but once Disney had obtained the serial rights (and moreover those of *Pinocchio* were free) nobody could charge him with unfaithfulness – and authors who have sold the rights of their novels to Hollywood can at most quarrel with the director if they feel that the movie does not match their original intentions.

On the other hand, if I were a British publisher and asked for a new translation of *Pinocchio*, and the translator gave me back a text starting with *Two households, both alike in dignity in fair Verona*, I would have the right to refuse the translation. In translation proper there is an implicit law, that is, the ethical obligation to respect what the author has written. It has been said that translation is a disguised indirect discourse ('The author so and so said in his/her language so and so'). Obviously, to establish exactly what 'the author said' is an interesting problem not only from a semantic point of view but also in terms of jurisprudence, as we shall see.

I dare to say (and I hope not to trouble some simple soul) that in order to define translation proper one must even take into account economic criteria. When I buy or look for a translation in a library that a great poet made of another great poet, I am not expecting something literally similar to the original; usually I look for a poetic translation because I already know the original and I want to see how the translator has challenged and emulated his source in his own language. When I watch the movie *Un maledetto imbroglio* by Pietro Germi, even though I know it is 'freely' inspired by Gadda's *Quer pasticciaccio brutto de via Merulana*, I do not believe that, since I have seen the movie, I can avoid reading the book (unless I am particularly underdeveloped). I do presume to find in the movie many elements of the story, some psychological features of the characters, certain Roman atmospheres, but certainly none of the linguistic inventions that made Gadda famous.

If, on the other hand, I buy an Italian translation of *David Copperfield* I assume that – at least in *some* way – the translation will not only tell me the original story but will also be able to suggest by its style that the events and the dialogues take place in nineteenth-century London and not during the Roman Empire or in a sort of Star Trek universe. The following essays will try to establish what I mean by 'in some way'.

Reading the translation of *David Copperfield* I would consider any cut as dishonest (I would call it censorship) and I would protest if I discovered that the translator made some characters say the contrary of what they said in Dickens's novel.

It is useless to object that these are mere commercial criteria or simple publishing conventions. Such legal and commercial criteria always hold even for artistic masterpieces. I would hazard a guess that when Michelangelo was asked to build the dome of St Peter's it was understood both by the buyer and the artist that that dome not only had to be beautiful but also had to endure. The perfection of function is one of the requirements of an art work.

It seems that to respect what the author said means to remain faithful to the original text. I understand how outdated such an expression can sound, when so many translation theories stress the principle according to which, in the translating process, the impact a translation has upon its own cultural milieu is more important than an impossible equivalence with the original. But the concept of faithfulness depends on the belief that translation is a form of interpretation and that (even while considering the cultural habits of their presumed readers) translators must aim at rendering, not necessarily the intention of the author (who may have been dead for millennia), but the *intention of the text* – the intention of the text being the outcome of an interpretative effort on the part of the reader, the critic or the translator.[6]

It is not necessary to think of complex hermeneutic examples. Let us suppose that in a novel a character says, *You're just pulling my leg.* To render such an idiom in Italian by *stai solo tirandomi la gamba* or *tu stai menandomi per la gamba* would be literally correct but misleading. In Italian one should say *mi stai prendendo per il naso*, thus substituting an English leg with an Italian nose. If literally translated, the English expression, absolutely unusual in Italian, would make the reader suppose that the character (as well as the author) was inventing a provocative rhetorical figure – which is completely misleading as in English the expression is simply an idiom. By choosing *nose* instead of *leg* a translator puts the Italian reader in the same situation as the original English one. Thus only by being *literally unfaithful* can a translator succeed in being truly faithful to the source text. Which is (to redeem the triviality of my example) like echoing Saint Jerome, patron saint of translators, that in translating one should not translate *verbum e verbo sed sensum exprimere de sensu* (even though the notion of the right sense of a text, as we shall see, can imply some ambiguities).

Besides, in the course of my experiences as a translated author I have always been torn between the need to have a translation that respected what I believed to be my intentions, and the exciting discovery that my text, independently of my early intentions, could elicit unexpected interpretations and be in some way improved when it was re-embodied in another language.

I do not need to develop these points in depth at this stage because the following pages will reveal them. What I want to emphasise is that many concepts circulating in translation studies (such as adequacy, equivalence, faithfulness) will be considered in the course of my lectures from the point of view of *negotiation*.

Negotiation is a process by virtue of which, in order to get something, each party renounces something else, and at the end everybody feels satisfied since one cannot have everything.

In this kind of negotiation there may be many parties: on one side, there is the original text, with its own rights, sometimes an author who claims right over the whole process, along with the cultural framework in which the original text is born; on the other side, there is the destination text, the cultural milieu in which it is expected to be read, and even the publishing industry, which can recommend different translation criteria, according to whether the translated text is to be put in an academic context or in a popular one. An English publisher of detective novels may even ask a Russian translator not to transliterate the names of the characters by using diacritic marks, in order to make them more recognisable to the supposed readers.

A translator is the negotiator between those parties, whose explicit assent is not mandatory. There is an implicit assent even in the reading of a novel or of a newspaper article, as in the former case the reader implicitly subscribes a *suspension of disbelief*, and in the latter relies on the silent convention that what is said is guaranteed to be true.

A last remark. The chapters of this book were born as lectures and when lecturing one does not include bibliographical references, except for canonical authors. Moreover a reasonable bibliography on translation studies today would contain hundreds of titles. I have only put footnotes where I felt in debt to an author for a particular suggestion. But I have refrained from tracing the origin of many other ideas because they are now current.[7]

NOTES

1. Now published as *Experiences in Translation* (Toronto: Toronto U. P., 2001).
2. A more consistent version of both my Toronto and Oxford lectures, including many other reflections and examples, is now published in Italian under the title of *Dire quasi la stessa cosa* (Milano: Bompiani, 2003).
3. Raymond Queneau, *Esercizi di stile* (Torino: Einaudi, 1983).
4. Gérard de Nerval, *Sylvie* (Torino: Einaudi, 1999).
5. Since I shall repeatedly quote some of these translations, let me provide the references here: *Le nom de la rose*, tr. Jean-Noel Schifano (Paris: Grasset, 1982); *Der Name der Rose*, tr. Burckhart Kroeber (München: Hanser, 1982); *El nombre de la rosa*, tr. Ricardo Pochtar (Barcelona: Lumen, 1982); *The Name of the Rose*, tr. William Weaver (New York: Harcourt/London: Secker and Warburg, 1983). *Le pendule de Foucault*, tr. Jean-Noel Schifano (Paris: Grasset, 1990); *Das Foucaultsche Pendel*, tr. Burckhart Kroeber (München: Hanser, 1989); *El pendolo de Foucault*, tr. Ricardo Pochtar and Helena Lozano Miralles (Barcelona: Lumen-Bompiani, 1989); *El pendel de Foucault*, tr. Antoni Vicens (Barcelona: Destino, 1989); *Foucault's Pendulum*, tr. William Weaver (New York: Harcourt/London: Secker and Warburg, 1989). *L'île du jour d'avant*, tr. Jean-Noel Schifano (Paris: Grasset, 1996); *Die Insel des vorigen Tages*, tr. Burckhart Kroeber (München: Hanser, 1995); *La isla del dia de antes*, tr. Helena Lozano Miralles (Barcelona: Lumen, 1995); *L'illa del dia abans*, tr. Antoni Vicens (Barcelona: Destino, 1995); *The Island of the Day Before*, tr. William Weaver (New York: Harcourt/London: Secker and Warburg, 1995). As for *Baudolino*, always with the same title, see the translations of Jean-Noel Schifano (Paris: Grasset, 2002), Burckhart Kroeber (München: Hanser, 2001), Helena Lozano Miralles (Barcelona: Lumen, 2001), Carmen Arenas Noguera (Barcelona: Destino, 2001), Marco

Lucchesi (Rio de Janeiro: Record, 2001), William Weaver (New York: Harcourt/London: Secker and Warburg, 2002).

6. Cf. my *The Role of the Reader* (Bloomington: Indiana a U.P., 1979 and London: Hutchinson, 1981) and *The Limits of Interpretation* (Bloomington: Indiana U.P., 1990).

7. See also for a consistent bibliography Mona Baker, ed., *Routledge Encyclopedia of Translation Studies* (London: Routledge, 1998).

ONE

The plants of Shakespeare

When I look in *Webster's Dictionary*, among the definitions of *translate* I find 'to transfer or turn from one set of symbols into another'. That is more or less what happens when we use Morse code and we translate from alphabetic letters to Morse signals or vice versa.

However Morse code involves a process of *transliteration*, that is, of substituting letters of a given alphabet with letters of another one, and letters are meaningless. Using Morse code, operators could correctly translate messages written in a language they do not understand into a series of dots and dashes. But *Webster's*, under the entry *translation*, also says 'a rendering from one language into another'. Since the signs of any language (be it verbal or other) signify something and are thus endowed with meaning, we can figure out that, given a set of symbols *a*, *b*, *c*, . . . *z* and another set of symbols α, β, γ, δ, . . . ω, we are entitled to substitute an item from the first set with an item from the second set if and only if, according to some rule of synonymity, *a* is equivalent in meaning to α, *b* to β, and so on.

What does 'equivalence in meaning' mean? There is a widespread opinion that meaning is exactly that which remains unchanged (or equivalent) in the process of translation, but such an assumption runs the risk of entering a vicious circle. Another suggestion[1] is that the equivalence implied by synonymity and translation is a *referential equivalence*: a given word A used in a language Alpha is synonymous with the word B used in a language Beta if both are seen to refer to the same thing or event in the real world. However, referential equivalence is no better than equivalence in meaning. We generally believe that it is correct to translate *husband* as *mari* or *marito*, and undoubtedly *Mary's husband* refers to the same person as *le mari de*

Mary or *il marito di Mary*. But one only need open a dictionary in order to see that *husband,* in English, can also mean a navy manager or a steward, while *mari* or *marito* cannot.

Let us assume, however, that synonymity exists, that equivalence in meaning is a value rigidly established by a linguistic convention, and that a machine can be provided with rules that allow it to operate according to that convention, so that it can switch from one symbol to another even though it does not understand the meaning of these symbols.

With this in mind, I accessed Babelfish, the automatic translation system provided by AltaVista (http://babelfish.altavista.com). I gave it a series of English expressions and asked it to translate them into Italian. Then I asked AltaVista to retranslate the Italian expressions back into English. Only in the last case did I follow a more complicated path, that is: English–Italian–German–English. Here are the results:

1. The works of Shakespeare → *Gli impianti di Shakespeare* → The plants of Shakespeare
2. Speaker of the chamber of deputies → *Altoparlante dell'alloggiamento dei delegati* → Loudspeaker of the lodging of the delegates
3. Studies in the logic of Charles Sanders Peirce → *Studi nella logica delle sabbiatrici Peirce del Charles* → Studien in der Logik der Charlessandpapierschleifmaschinen Peirce → Studies in the logic of the Charles of sanders paper grinding machines Peirce

Let us stick to case number 1. AltaVista undoubtedly has definitions and dictionary translations in its 'mind' (if AltaVista has a mind of any description), because it is true that the English word *work* can be translated into Italian as *impianti* and the Italian *impianti* can be translated into English as *plants*. Plainly we must give up the idea that *to translate* means only 'to transfer or turn from one set of symbols into another' because, except for cases of transliteration like Morse code, a given word in a natural language Alpha frequently has more than one corresponding term in the natural language Beta. Besides, the problem does not only concern translation but also the very comprehension of a language Alpha on the part of its native speakers. What does *work* mean in English? According to *Webster's*, work can be an activity, a task, a duty, the result of such activity (such as a work of art or a literary masterpiece), a structure in engineering (such as a fort, a bridge, a tunnel), a place where industrial labour is carried out (like a plant or a factory) – and many other things. Thus, if we accept the idea of equivalence in meaning, we could say that *work* is synonymous and equivalent in meaning both with *literary masterpiece* and with *factory*.

When a single word can express two different things or concepts we no longer speak of synonymity but rather of *homonymy*. We have synonymity when two terms both refer to the same thing or concept, but we have homonymy when a single term refers to two different things or concepts.

If a lexicon contained only synonyms (and if synonymity was an unambiguous concept), then translation would be possible, even for AltaVista. If in the same lexicon there are many homonyms then translation becomes a discombobulating job.

I know that the notion of meaning is a very complicated one and I would like to avoid it. Let me assume that what we naively call the meaning of a word is everything in a dictionary (or better, an encyclopaedia) that is written in the corresponding entry for that word.

Every single thing written in that entry is part of the content expressed by that word. If we read the content of a given entry we realise that (a) it includes many accepted meanings or senses (the case of the word *work* is a very clear example), and (b) these senses are not always expressed by an alleged synonym but by a definition, a paraphrase or a concrete example. In this sense a dictionary provides a series of interpretations for a given word, or, according to Charles Sanders Peirce,[2] of *interpretants* of that sign.

For Peirce, an interpretant is another representation which refers to the same 'object'. In order to tell the content of an expression (be it verbal or other) we must substitute the first expression with another expression (or string of expressions), which in its turn can be interpreted by another expression (or string of expressions).

An interpretant can be a synonym (in those rare cases in which one can believe in synonymity, as happens with *husband, mari, marito*); a sign from another semiotic system (the word *work* can be interpreted by showing the photograph of an engineering structure); a given object which is shown as representative of the class to which it belongs (one can interpret the word *work* by indicating a real engineering structure); a definition; a description; a paraphrase; or a complex discourse that inferentially develops all the logical possibilities implied by the content of the expression. For instance, if one takes into account that there is something in common between the various senses of *work*, since a literary masterpiece, a bridge, a factory, and a painting are all artificial objects made by human beings by virtue of an activity or labour, and that the same senses are conveyed by the Latin word *opus*, then even this complex inference is an interpretant of the expression *work*.

Certainly a dictionary (as a concrete object sold in bookstores) does not provide all the possible interpretants of a given linguistic term – this is the job of an ideal encyclopaedia. But even a dictionary at least tries to circumscribe the sense that a given term assumes in the more frequently recurrent contexts. Lexicographers, if they know their job, not only provide definitions; they also provide instructions for contextual disambiguation, and this helps a lot in choosing the most adequate term in another language.

According to Peirce, every interpretation teaches us something more about the content of the interpreted expression. 'Feline mammal', '*Felis catus*' and 'domestic animal which miaows' are certainly three different interpretations of the expression *cat*, but the first suggests a property (to be viviparous) that the second does not, and the third tells us something about the way to recognise a cat that the first did not provide. At the same time every interpretation focuses on the interpreted content from a different point of view. Thus all the interpretations of the same expression cannot be mutually synony-mous, and every expression resembles a homonymous term conveying a different interpretation.

Moreover, in certain cases, we are facing examples of real homonymy, as happens with the very famous example of *bachelor*. This term can be translated as *soltero, scapolo, célibataire* only within a human context, possibly concerning questions of marriage. Within a university context a bachelor is a person who has received a bachelor's degree (therefore it becomes a *diplomato* or improperly a *laureato* in Italian, or a *licencié* in French), and in a medieval context a *bachelor* is 'a young knight who follows the banner of another' – that is, in Italian, a *baccelliere*. Within a zoological context, a bachelor is 'a male animal, like a seal, without a mate during breeding time'. It is because of these contextual selections that, if I am given the English text *John, a bachelor, who studied at Oxford, is now writing a Ph.D. dissertation on the North Pole bachelors*, I should not translate it into French as *Jean, une foque sans copine qui s'est licenciée à Oxford, est en train d'écrire une thèse de doctorat sur les célibataires du Pole Nord...*[3]

At this point we can understand why AltaVista's Babelfish is doomed to be wrong. It is not endowed with a vocabulary that includes contextual selections (or that can interpret them with sufficient precision). Thus AltaVista was unable to realise that the word *work* has one sense in a literary context and another in an industrial one. Or maybe AltaVista was endowed with the necessary information that *works* in literature means a series of texts or books, but it did not receive any information that the phrase to be translated concerned literature. In order to realise it, AltaVista would have had to know that Shakespeare was a poet and a playwright and not an industrial tycoon. This is the kind of information that is not usually provided by dictionaries, but by encyclopaedias.

Is it conceivable that AltaVista was not provided with contextual information? Perhaps it simply needs a larger context, so that it can find therein useful information in order to disambiguate the most puzzling expressions. In order to test this theory I chose a more consistent and very well-known text:

In the beginning God created the heaven and the earth; and the earth was without form, and void; and darkness was upon the face of the deep. And the Spirit of God moved upon the face of the waters; and God said, Let there be Light, and there was Light. And God saw the Light, that it was good: and God divided the Light from the darkness. And God called the Light Day, and the darkness he called Night. And the evening and the morning were the first day. And God said, Let there be a firmament in the midst of the waters, and let it divide the waters from the waters. And God made the firmament, and divided the waters which were under the firmament from the waters which were above the firmament. And it was so.

I asked AltaVista to translate it into Spanish, and I got in return:

*En el dios **que comenzaba** creó el cielo y la tierra y la tierra **estaban** sin forma, y **vacío**; y la oscuridad estaba sobre la **cara** del profundo. Y el **alcohol del dios** se movió sobre la **cara** de las aguas. Y el dios dijo, dejó allí ser luz: y había luz. Y el dios vio la luz, de **que que** era bueno: y el dios dividió la luz de la oscuridad. Y el dios llamó el día **ligero**, y la oscuridad que él llamó **a Noche**. Y la tarde y la mañana eran el primer día. Y el dios dijo, dejó allí ser un **firmament** en el medio de las aguas, y lo dejó dividir las aguas de las aguas. Y el dios hizo el firmament, y dividió las aguas que estaban bajo el firmament de las aguas que estaban sobre el firmament. **Y estaba tan**.*

AltaVista cannot be blamed if it interpreted *God called the Light Day* as the story of a god who summoned a weightless day; likewise, the idea of interpreting *void* as a noun and not as an adjective can be considered a minor flaw. AltaVista had the right to interpret *face* as *cara* (in English it would be *countenance*) and not as *surface*: why should the abyss have a surface and not a countenance, like the Moon? At most AltaVista should have detected that *that it* cannot be translated as *que que*, but nobody is perfect.

Altavista read *beginning* not as a noun but as an adjective, but I had never supposed that it was endowed with the biblical and theological competence necessary to be able to distinguish between a god who is there at the beginning and a god who is on the verge of starting something. Besides, even from a theological and cosmological point of view, this *Dios que comenzaba* is moving and convincing. As far as we know, it really was the first time He was creating a world, and perhaps this explains many imperfections of our universe, including the difficulties of translation.

It seems that AltaVista is not endowed with information about contextual selections or rules of contextual disambiguation because it was unable to realise that *spirit* acquires a given meaning when uttered or written in a church and another one when uttered or written in a pub. Why did it not know this? The answer is easy: it did not realise that the name *God* implies spiritual and not profane matters because in its vocabulary the name God *was not interpreted*. AltaVista probably has merely a list of correspondences, like Morse code (that is, a list of alleged synonyms). Thus it is not entitled to know anything about God.

To continue my game, I asked Altavista to retranslate the Spanish text into English, and was given:

> In the God **that began** created the sky and the Earth and the Earth was **without form, and emptiness**; and the dark was on the face of the deep one. And **the alcohol of the God** moved on the face of waters. There and the God said, let be light: and there was light. And the God saw the light, **that that** was good: and the God divided **the light of the dark**. And the God called the **slight day**, and the dark that it called **to Night**. And afternoon and the morning was the first day. And the God said, there it let be firmament **in means** of waters, **and it let divide it waters of waters**. And the God did firmament, and divided the waters that were under firmament **of the** waters that were on firmament. And it was so.

This text is more or less a victim of the misunderstandings of the Spanish version, plus some new mistakes (for instance it translates the

Spanish *medio*, middle, as *means*). Notice that, faced with the Spanish expression *dividir las aguas de las aguas*, AltaVista, if provided with a reasonable dictionary, should have detected that the Spanish preposition *de* can be translated either as *of* or *from*. AltaVista nonchalantly chose *of* because it lacks the fundamental information that, in the world we live in, there is nothing like *waters of waters*. This is not a mere piece of encyclopaedia information, like the facts that Shakespeare was an author and that God is a spiritual being. It concerns our understanding of the world. Let me avoid a painful semiotic discussion over whether an understanding of the world should or should not be included within an encyclopaedic competence. We shall see later that there are certain pieces of information about the world which are not registered by an encyclopaedia but rather provided on the spot by a given text (like *there is a cat on the mat*). However, we have succeeded in adding a new stricture to our criteria for good translating competence: translation does not only concern words and language in general but also the world, or at least the possible world described by a given text.

At this point I decided that, by continuing to play, I could probably get some other interesting suggestions, so I asked AltaVista to translate the English text into German, which produced this:

Im Gott, **der anfing, stellte** *den Himmel und die* **Masse** *und die* **Masse** *war ohne* **Formular und emptiness her;** *und die Dunkelheit war auf dem* **Gesicht** *vom tiefen. Und der* **Spiritus** *des Gottes verschob sich auf dem Gesicht des Wassers. Dort und der Gott sagte,* **lassend Sie,** *Licht zu sein: und es gab Licht. Und der Gott sah das Licht,* **das, das** *gut war: und der Gott teilte das Licht* **der** *Dunkelheit. Und der Gott benannte den* **geringfügigen** *Tag und die Dunkelheit, die sie zur Nacht benannte. Und Nachmittag und der Morgen waren der erste Tag. Und der Gott sagte,* **dort ließ er** *firmament in* **den Mitteln** *des Wassers sein, und er ließ es teilen* **wässert** *vom Wasser. Und der Gott tat firmament und teilte das Wasser, das unter firmament des Wassers waren, das auf firmament waren. Und es war so.*

The German text accepts the story of a beginning God, of the light day, of a world without void, and *that that* obviously becomes *das das*. But it mistranslates *Earth* as *Mass*, *form* as *formular*, and the divine alcohol becomes *Spiritus*, which is as ambiguous as *spirit*. There are other syntactical oddities. In order to translate *created* AltaVista finds the German verb *herstelle*, which must be conjugated as *Ich stelle her* or *Ich stellte her*. Because of a syntactic rule that was provided, AltaVista 'knows' that *her* should be put at the end of the sentence, but it does not realise that the sentence already ended with *Himmel*, and so put *her* much too far ahead. Moreover, apropos *waters of waters*, the first term is interpreted as a verb and the second as a noun. Such a mishmash could not but give the following result when I asked the computer to retranslate German into English:

> In the God, which began, **placed** the sky and the **mass** and the **mass** was without form and emptiness **ago**; and the darkness was on the face of the deep. And the **white spirits** of the God shifted on the face of the water. There and the God said, **leaving you**, to be light: and there was light. And the God saw the light, **which, which** was good: and the God divided **the light of the darkness**. And the God **designated the slight day** and the darkness, which **designated it to the night**. And afternoon and the morning were the first day and the God said, there let it **in the means** of the water be firmament, and it left it divides **waessert** from the water. And the God did firmament and divided the water, which firmament **under the water was**, which were on firmament. And it was like that.

It is interesting to remark that, faced with *stellte . . . her*, AltaVista does not (and with good reason) recognise a compound verb; it finds in its dictionary that *her* alone can also mean *ago*; and concocts *placed . . . ago*. (By way of compensation, many other verbs are put at the end of the sentence, as in *under the water was*.) *Spiritus* again becomes something alcoholic, and the program is unable to translate *waessert*.

The conclusion of my experiment is that in order to translate, one must know a lot of things, most of them independent of mere grammatical competence.

But at this point we are encouraged towards another reflection. If one received the different versions of Genesis provided by Babelfish, one would guess that they were bad translations of the King James text – and not, let us say, bad versions of the first adventure of Harry Potter. And if someone who had never heard of the Bible read these versions, I think that even such a naive reader would in some way realise that these texts deal with a God who has created a world (even if it would be very difficult to understand what the hell He actually made).

When I started working for a publishing house I was given the manuscript of a translation from English for a first check, without being able to refer to the English original, which was still in the hands of the translator. The book told the story of the first researches on the atomic bomb in America, and at a certain point it said that, gathered in a certain place, a group of young scientists had started their work by performing *corse di treni* (which in English means *train races*). I thought it was pretty peculiar that persons who were supposed to discover the secrets of the atom wasted their precious time in such childish play. I resorted to my world knowledge and inferred that these scientists were certainly doing something else. I do not remember whether at this point I remembered an English expression that I already knew, or tried to retranslate the Italian expression into English as if I were a bad translator. In any case I immediately realised that these scientists were on *training courses*, which was more reasonable and less expensive for American taxpayers. As soon as I received the English original I saw that I was right, and I did my best to get the translator fired immediately.

Another time, in the translation of a psychology book, I found that, in the course of an experiment, *l'ape riuscì a prendere la banana posta fuori dall sua gabbia aiutandosi con un bastone,* that is: a bee succeeded in grasping a banana lying outside its cage with the help of a stick.

My first reaction drew on world knowledge: bees are unable to grasp bananas with a stick. My second reaction used linguistic knowledge. If one cross-references the Italian and English a 'false friend' is revealed:

ITALIAN	ENGLISH
Ape	Bee
Scimmione	Ape

It was clear that the original English text spoke of an *ape* and that the translator believed that *ape* meant *bee* in English too. Furthermore, my encyclopaedic knowledge was telling me that apes do grasp and eat bananas.

All this means that, even if a translation is wrong, not only is it possible to recognise the text that it translates badly, but a reasonable interpreter can usually infer, from a wrong translation of an unknown original, what that original was probably saying.

Every text (even the most simple sentence) describes or presupposes a possible world. In the two cases above I made some inferences about the world described by the text, by comparing it with the world we are living in, and trying to figure out how an atomic scientist and a bee should behave. After having made a hypothesis about the probable structure of the world pictured by the original text, a short exploration into the English lexicon helped me to find a reasonable final hypothesis: the scientists were on training courses and the banana was grasped by an ape.

Another example: in Italian we have only one word (*nipote*) for the three English words *nephew*, *niece* and *grandchild*. Moreover in English the possessive adjective agrees with the gender of the possessor while in Italian it agrees with the gender of the possessed object or person. Now suppose we have to translate the phrase *John visita ogni giorno sua sorella Ann per vedere suo nipote Sam*. The possible English translations are:

1. Every day John visits his sister Ann to see his nephew Sam.
2. Every day John visits his sister Ann to see her nephew Sam.

3. Every day John visits his sister Ann to see her grandchild Sam.
4. Every day John visits his sister Ann to see his grandchild Sam.

The last translation seems less probable than the previous ones, but it is possible to imagine a world in which (i) John had a son, Max, (ii) Max married Mary, (iii) Max and Mary gave birth to Sam, (iv) they then died in a car accident, (v) aunt Ann decided to adopt Sam. A very improbable but not impossible world situation (given the present corruption of any moral principle) would be that Max, son of John, had a love affair with his aunt Mary, and that they produced Sam, so that Sam can be correctly defined both as John's grandchild and as John's nephew. In any case, if the general context does not provide translators with further information, so that they can conceive of a possible world structure, it is impossible to translate that Italian sentence on mere linguistic grounds.

In order to understand a text, or at least in order to decide how it should be translated, translators have to figure out the possible world pictured by that text. Often they can only make a hypothesis about that possible world. This means that a translation is also the result of a conjecture or of a series of conjectures. Once the most reasonable conjecture has been made, the translators should make their linguistic decisions accordingly. Thus given the whole spectrum of the content displayed by the dictionary entry (plus all the necessary encyclopaedic information), translators must choose the most suitable or relevant meaning or *sense* for that context.

You have probably realised that I started speaking of differences between languages (in the sense of tongues) and now I am speaking of differences between texts. This is a very crucial point for every translation theory. But let me go on with languages.

These are two main arguments against translation, both more germane than they seem at first sight: (i) the impossibility of setting up a unique translation manual and (ii) the incommensurability of language structures.

As for the first argument, following Quine's famous example, it is difficult to establish the meaning of a term in an unknown language even when the two speakers are facing the same external stimulus – which casts in doubt the notion of referential equivalence. If the linguist points to a passing rabbit and the native informant utters *gavagai!* it is uncertain whether, by that expression, the native speaker means rabbit, stages of rabbit, or the fact that an animal is passing through the grass at that moment – or whether *gavagai* is the proper name of a universal rabbithood. It is impossible to decide, if one has no previous information on the native culture – that is, if one does not know how the natives categorise things, parts of things, or events involving things. The linguist must start by making a series of analytical hypotheses in order finally to produce a translation manual that corresponds to a whole anthropological handbook. However, the indeterminacy of translation is proven by the fact that rival systems of analytical hypotheses can produce different (but equally legitimate) translations of the same sentence. In Quine's words, 'Just as we meaningfully speak of the truth of a sentence only within the terms of some theory or conceptual scheme ... so on the whole we may meaningfully speak of interlinguistic synonymy only within the terms of some particular system of analytical hypotheses.'[4]

In spite of the current cliché about the incompatibility between Anglo-Saxon and Continental philosophy, I believe that Quinean holism is not so different from the idea that every language has its own genius (as Humboldt said) or – better – that every language expresses a different world view (the Sapir–Whorf hypothesis). In what sense a given language designs its own world view is pretty clearly explained by the structural semiotics of Hjelmslev.[5] According to Hjelmslev, a natural language (and, more generally, any semiotic system) consists of a plane of expression and a plane of content which represents the universe of the concepts that can be expressed by that language. Each of these planes consists of form and substance and both are the result of the organisation of a pre-linguistic continuum.

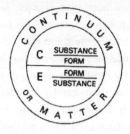

If we consider the English language, the form of expression consists of its phonological system, its lexical repertory and its syntactic rules. Through this form of expression, we may generate various substances of expression, such as the words we utter every day. But I shall speak of substances in another essay. Let me consider here the problem of form. In order to elaborate a form of expression, English has selected (from the continuum of the sounds that the human voice can produce) a series of sounds, excluding others that exist and are pronounceable but which do not belong to the English language.

If the sounds of a language are to be comprehensible it is necessary to associate them with contents. For Hjelmslev, the continuum of content is the totality of all that can be thought and said: namely the whole universe, physical and mental (as far as we can speak of it), including the material elements such as sounds that we use to make expressions. Each language organises the universe of what may be said and thought into a *form*. The system of colours, the organisation of the zoological universe in genera, families and species, the opposition of high vs low, and even the structures that linguists identify in phonological systems – all belong to the form of content. Certain cultures organise the kinship system by isolating differences that in Great Britain, as well as in Italy, are ignored: for instance, the difference between the brother of the mother and the brother of the father, who for us are both uncles.

In this sense two semantic systems can result in being mutually inaccessible, because they segment the content continuum in a different way. Thus, according to Quine, one cannot translate the

expression *neutrinos lack mass* into a jungle language, and one only
need think how difficult it is to translate the German word *Sehnsucht*
into English or Italian in order to understand that German culture has
the precise notion of a certain passion whose 'semantic space' can be
only partially covered by terms like *nostalgia, yearning, craving for* or
wishfulness (and none of them renders it adequately).

But frequently such inadequacy is only the result of a sort of
'optical effect'. Let us return for a moment to the distinction between
nephew/niece and grandson. It is clear that where English recognises
three separate content entities, Italian recognises only one: *nipote*.

ENGLISH	ITALIAN
Nephew	
Niece	Nipote
Grandchild	

Now, it is true that in Italian a single word is used to express three
different units deriving from the segmentation of the continuum of
kinship relationships. But this graphic representation of the phenomenon can be very misleading if we imagine that the four words
(*nephew, niece, grandchild* and *nipote*) represent concepts, or content
units. They *do* represent *words*, which are used to mean a certain
content unit, and curiously Italian has one word for three distinct
positions in the kinship system. But the fact that there is only one
word does not mean that Italians do not see any difference between
the child of one's son or daughter and the child of one's sister or
brother. They see it to such an extent that even in the case of death
duties the two kinds of relatives pay a different tax. This means that
Italians have more linguistic difficulties than speakers of other
languages in certain contexts where the distinction between nephew/
niece and grandchild becomes relevant.

Despite having only one word, then, Italians conceive three
content units, and these units, which are not distinguished from each
other by a specific word, are nonetheless interpreted by dictionaries or
encyclopaedias, which explain what I have just explained – namely,

the difference in kinship between a niece and a grandchild. To translate means to see, under the words, the possible interpretation of these slots, which are not conceptually empty but only linguistically ill-named.

ENGLISH TERMS	CONTENT	ITALIAN TERMS
Nephew	Son of the brother or sister	
Niece	Daughter of the brother or sister	Nipote
Grandchild	Son or daughter of the son or daughter	

To be honest, since there are different kinship systems, more finely segmented, one could say that even English is very savage in comparison with a jungle language that has more names for different kinship positions. For example:

ENGLISH TERMS	CONTENT	TERMS OF JUNGLE LANGUAGE X
	Son of the brother	Term A
Nephew	Son of the sister	Term B
	Daughter of the brother	Term C
Niece	Daughter of the sister	Term D
	Son or daughter of the son	Term E
Granchild	Son or daughter of the daughter	Term F

But this does not prove that an English speaker is unable to recognise the different kinship positions expressed in our jungle language by the series of terms A–F. English speakers have no names for these different positions but are able to interpret each of them correctly.

The challenge for a translator, when two languages seem to have a different segmentation of the content continuum, is to make a reasonable conjecture about the content space covered by a homonym term in a given context.

Up to this point I have argued as if translation were a process taking place between tongues, that is, between two different linguistic systems. It is not so, otherwise the paramount example of translation would be a bilingual dictionary. On the contrary, students taking an exam in a foreign language are not expected to produce a dictionary. They are requested to use (or to know by heart) a dictionary in order correctly to translate *a text*.

We must come back to the structure of a natural language. The diagram on page 22 suggested that form, substance and continuum were all elements of the structure of a language, and they were put in that diagram in order to show how they are mutually related.

In fact the study of a linguistic system starts when a given language has already segmented the continuum of all possible sounds into a form of expression, and the same happens with the content. In this sense the study of a language as a system is concerned only with forms: content form and expression form.

Substance is not a system phenomenon. It appears only when, by exploiting the possibilities provided by a given linguistic system, one *physically* produces a *text* or, if you prefer, a *discourse*. The substance of an expression is produced, materially, only when a communication process begins, that is, when sounds are emitted according to the rules of a given language.

Translation is a phenomenon which does not concerrn the relationships between two languages or linguistic systems – except in the rare cases in which one asks native speakers or interpreters how they would translate a given term in their own language, and we have seen what we risk by asking a native of Quine or the programmer of Babelfish. Rather, translation is a process that takes place between two texts produced at a given historical moment in a given cultural milieu.

One can adequately translate the Italian word *nipote* into English only when it occurs within an expressed text, referring to a given possible world or state of affairs. Otherwise one cannot make any reasonable decision.

Thus in a text, which is a *produced* substance, we have a Linear Text Manifestation – like the words I uttered at Oxford or these you are reading on this page – and the Sense or the multiple Senses of that given text: not the multiple meanings of the word *nipote* but the sense that this word acquires in a given context.

When I start interpreting a Linear Text Manifestation, I rely on the whole of my linguistic knowledge, and a more complex process occurs when I try to elicit the sense of what is said. As a first approach I try to understand the literal sense of the single sentences (if they are not ambiguous, hence requiring the help of a wider context), and to see them as referring to a given possible world. If I read that Snow White is eating an apple I know that a female individual is biting, chewing and swallowing a fruit, and I can make some hypotheses about the possible world where this scene occurs: is it a world like the one we live in, where an apple a day keeps the doctor away, or a fairy-tale universe where to eat an apple means to become the victim of a spell? If I choose the second possibility, then I have to resort to encyclopaedic competences, among which there are intertextual *scripts*, explaining that in fairy tales things usually happen in a certain fashion. Naturally I am obliged to explore the Linear Manifestation further in order to know something more about Snow White, as well as about the place and the time in which the events occur.

At every step of my reading I ask myself what the *topic* is of a sentence, of a paragraph or of a whole chapter, and I must isolate *isotopies*, that is, homogeneous sense levels.

At this point I would be able to reconstruct a story from the plot, the story being the chronological sequence of events that can be turned upside down or at least 'edited' by the plot. I can tell the story of Little Red Riding Hood, for instance, starting from the end, with the girl who, after having being rescued by the hunter, remembers what happened in the early morning when she met the wolf for the first time, and step by step reconstructs her vicissitudes.

By the way, notice that such a distinction also holds for non-fictional texts. *I hated John, so I killed him* and *Since I hated John I killed him* are two Linear Manifestations that convey the same story with two different plots. Moreover, story and plot also hold for non-narrative texts. Take a poem like 'A Silvia' by Leopardi. There is a story: there was a young woman, the poet secretly loved her, she died, and the poet remembers her in the flower of her youth, as well as his lost illusions. But this story is seen through a plot: the poet shows up when his illusions are definitively lost, and the young woman appears as a gentle ghost in the midst of his desperate remembrances. In translating 'A Silvia' one should respect not only the story but also the plot; otherwise one would concoct not a translation of this delicate poem but rather a clumsy summary.

Because I try to reconstruct the story from the plot, as my reading goes on, I will transform large textual chunks (or series of sentences and paragraphs) into micro-propositions that recapitulate them – at the middle of my reading of *Snow White* I can synthesise what I learned as 'Snow White is a beautiful young princess who arouses the jealousy of her stepmother who wants her to be killed in the woods', but at a further stage of the tale I can sum up the whole story by a macro-proposition as 'A persecuted beautiful young princess is received and welcomed by seven dwarves.' This embedding from micro- to macro-propositions will be my way to isolate the 'deep' story of the whole tale, and even its moral meaning (if any), while at the same time deciding which events can be considered as essential and which ones marginal or parenthetic.

Then I can try to detect the psychological features of the characters, and their position in what Greimas calls *actantial structures*,[6] in the sense that many different characters can play the role of the Opponent or the Helper, and a given character can seem at the beginning to be the Helper and then become the Opponent (such a strategy is for instance typical of detective stories, where a character seems to collaborate with the detective until, in the last chapter, he/she is revealed as the culprit, that is, the detective's arch-foe).

It would be possible to discover other textual levels that I can focus on during my reading. There is no fixed chronological progression (neither top-to-bottom nor bottom-up), in so far as at the very moment I try to detect the topic of a sentence, I can also try hypotheses about the great moral or ideological structures of the whole text – and once again detective stories are a useful touchstone because they usually show how a text can deceive its readers, persuading them to make wrong inferences about the general sense of certain events and to venture wrong guesses.

Any interpretative bet on the different levels of sense, and on their importance for the global interpretation of a text, is obviously fundamental for any reader, but it is essential for a translator. Another crucial point, however, is that a plurality of levels can also be found in the Linear Manifestation.

There are many substances in the Linear Manifestation. This is evident for many non-verbal systems: take for example a movie, where images certainly count for a lot, but one must also take into account rhythm, editing, sound (words or noises, and music), and even graphic elements – not only when there are subtitles, but also when the movie shows written expression, such as the title of a book or an advertisement that is visible in the background. In a painting we ought to consider not only the iconic elements but also colours and chiaroscuro relationships, not to mention an iconological lexicon allowing one to recognise a Christ, a Virgin, a Saint or a King.

In a verbal text, obviously the linguistic substance is the most evident one, but it is not always the most relevant. The expression *Would you like to close the door?* can express courtesy, love, rage, sadism or shyness, according to the tone in which it is uttered, but these feelings would be equally communicated if the expression were *please pass the butter.* All these are phenomena that linguistics considers as *suprasegmental* or *tonemic,* and which do not have directly to do with the laws of a linguistic system (one can express rage by uttering either *please pass the butter* or *prego, passami il burro*). If I say (and I apologise for offering you such a bad example of poetry) *Please pass the butter – that is what I utter*, I am making stylistical phenomena, metrical elements and rhyme pertinent. Metric is so independent from the linguistic system that the hendecasyllabic structure can be embodied by expression in different languages, and the problem for translators of poetry is to find something in their own language that can be considered equivalent to a rhyme in the source language.

To cite Leopardi's 'A Silvia' once again, any effort to translate its first strophe would be inadequate if it did not succeed (and it is usually impossible to succeed) in making the final word an anagram of the initial name (*Silvia/salivi*). It can only really be done if one changes the name of the girl, thus losing the various assonances and hidden alliterations in *i* that link the sound both of *Silvia* and *salivi* with *occhi tuoi ridenti* and *fuggitivi*. See a comparison between the original text, where I put the *i*s in bold type, and the French translation by Michel Orcel (where obviously one does not stress all the alphabetical *i*s that in French produce a different sound):[7]

Silvia, rimembri ancora
Quel tempo della tua vita mortale
Quando beltà splendea
Negli occhi tuoi ridenti e fuggitivi,
e tu, lieta e pensosa, il limitare
di gioventù salivi?

Sylvia, te souvient-il encore
Du temps de cette vie mortelle,
Quand la beauté brillait
Dans tes regards rieurs et fugitifs,
Et que tu t'avançais, heureuse et sage,
Au seuil de ta jeunesse?

Orcel has inevitably missed the relation between *Silvia* and *salivi*. He has succeeded in putting quite a few *i*s in his texts, but the ratio of French to Italian is ten to twenty. Moreover, in the original text these *is* are easy to notice because they are repeated six times in the body of a single word, while in French this happens only once. As a final defeat in the course of a brave contest, the Italian name *Silvia*, with its accent on the first *i*, protracts the subtle fascination of the name as well as of the named person, while the French *Sylvia* (since the lack of the tonic accent in French inexorably obliges the speaker – and the reader – to stress the final *a*) transforms a sigh into a lash.

To conclude, (i) a text is the manifestation of a substance, either at the content or at the expression plane, and (ii) translation is not only concerned with such matters as 'equivalence' in meaning (or in the substance of the textual content), it is also concerned with the more or less indispensable 'equivalences' in the substance of expression (as we shall see more clearly in the following essays). In translating we must isolate various substantial levels. An insensitive, inattentive or superficial reader may miss or disregard many of them: one can read a fairy tale to enjoy the story without paying attention to its moral meaning, one can read *Hamlet* purely in order to see if Hamlet will succeed in avenging his father, one can read 'A Silvia' simply in order to know if the poet married the girl in the end or found another sweetheart. Translators are in theory bound to identify each of the relevant textual levels, but they may be obliged to choose which ones to preserve, since it is impossible to save all.

If we consider that in poetic texts it is crucial to render a strict relationship between given levels of the expression substance and given levels of the content substance, translators are challenged on their ability to identify them, to save all of them (or some, or none), and to put them in the same relationship with each other as they are in the original text.

In this game, translators may miss a lot, but can also make up for some of their losses.

NOTES

1. See for instance Werner Koller, 'Equivalence in Translation Theory',

in Chestermann, A., ed., *Readings in Translation Theory* (Helsinki: Oy Finn Lectura AB, 1989).

2. My references to Peirce will always be to *Collected Papers* (Cambridge U.P., 1931–58).

3. As a matter of fact I gave the English sentence to AltaVista and received as an output: *John, un célibataire qui a étudié à Oxford, a écrit maintenant une dissertation de Ph.D. sur les célibataires de Pôle du nord.*

4. Willard Van Orman Quine, *Word and Object* (Cambridge U.P., 1960), vol. II, p. 16.

5. Louis Hjelmslev, *Prolegomena to a Theory of Language* (Madison: Wisconsin U.P., 1943).

6. Cf. Algirdas J. Greimas and Joseph Courtés, eds., *Semiotics and Language: An Analytical Dictionary* (Bloomington: Indiana U.P., 1982).

7. G. Leopardi, *Les chants*, tr. Michel Orcel (Lausanne: L'Age d'Homme, 1982).

TWO

Losses and gains

There is no exact way to translate the Latin word *mus* into English. In Latin *mus* covers the same semantic space covered by *mouse* and *rat* in English – as well as in French, where there are *souris* and *rat*, in Spanish (*ratón* and *rata*) or in German (*Maus* and *Ratte*). But in Italian, even though the difference between a *topo* and a *ratto* is recorded in dictionaries, in everyday language one can use *topo* even for a big rat – perhaps stretching it to *topone* or *topaccio* – but *ratto* is used only in technical texts.

LATIN	ENGLISH	FRENCH	GERMAN	ITALIAN
	Mouse	Souris	Maus	(Topo)
mus				topo
	Rat	Rat	Ratte	(Ratto)

Thus, a comparison between French and Italian linguistic systems tells us that the Italian *topo* can cover the semantic spaces of both the French *souris* and *rat*. It is an interesting piece of linguistic information, but what happens when we find the word *topo* in an Italian translation of a French text? Does it translate back as *rat* or *souris*?

Take the first chapter of Camus's *La peste* in the Italian translation by Beniamino dal Fabbro. It states that one morning Doctor Rieux found, on the stairs of the building, *un sorcio morto*. Now *sorcio* is like *topo*, and like *mouse* in English, and if one knows that *mouse* in French is *souris* one can infer that the Italian translator chose *sorcio* instead of *topo* because he was phonically influenced by the French *souris*. In spite of these obvious assumptions, one is tempted to reflect on the fact that Camus's novel is telling the story of a terrible epidemic, and the plague is not usually carried by mice but by rats. Thus, not because of one's linguistic competence but by virtue of a general knowledge concerning the world we live in, one is encouraged to suppose that the translator made a mistake. As a matter of fact, if you check the French original, you will see that Camus does not mention a mouse but *un rat*. This is an instance in which the Italian translator should have stressed the difference and mentioned, if not a *ratto*, at least a *grosso topo* or a *topo di chiavica*.

Now let us suppose that one has to translate *How now! A rat?* from *Hamlet* (Act III, scene iv) into Italian. As far as I know, every Italian version translates it as *Cosa c'è, un topo?* or *Come? Un topo?* A rigorous translator should check in an old dictionary whether in Shakespeare's time *rat* meant, as *Webster's* says today, 'any of numerous rodents (*Rattus* and related genera) differing from the related mice by considerably larger size and by structural details', adding that *a rat* can also be 'a contemptible person' (and that *to smell a rat* means to realise that there is a secret plot). In fact Shakespeare, at least in *Richard III*, used *rat* as an insult. However, in Italian the word *ratto* has no connotation of 'contemptible person', and rather suggests (though improperly) speed (*ratto* as an adjective means 'speedy'). Moreover, in every situation in which someone is frightened by a rodent (when, according to a vaudeville tradition, women jump upon a chair and men grasp a broom to kill the intruder) the usual scream is *un topo!* and not *un ratto!*

I decide that Hamlet, in order to kill Polonius, did not need to know if there was a *mouse* or a *rat* behind that arras, and that the word *topo* accurately suggests surprise, instinctive alarm, and an impulse to kill. For all these reasons I accept the usual translation: *Cosa c'è? Un topo?*

If in Camus's case it was indispensable to make the size of that rodent clear, and it had to be a rat, for the imagined animal in *Hamlet* it was more important to stress its sudden passage and the nervous reaction it elicited (and justified).

In making my decision I have not only relied upon definitions, contextual selections or long lists of interpretants provided by dictionaries and encyclopaedias. We have *negotiated* which portion of the expressed content was strictly pertinent in that given context.

This notion of negotiation will dominate my next essays. Between the purely theoretical argument that, since languages are differently structured, translation is impossible, and the commonsensical acknowledgement that people, in this world, after all, do translate and understand each other, it seems to me that the idea of translation as a process of negotiation (between author and text, between author and readers, as well as between the structure of two languages and the encyclopaedias of two cultures) is the only one that matches our experience.

When speaking of negotiation I do not mean to suggest a sort of deconstructionist idea according to which, since translation is a matter of negotiation, there are no lexical or textual rules that can be used as a parameter for telling an acceptable from a bad or incorrect translation. The possibility, and even the advisability of a negotiation does not exclude the presence of rules or of conventions. One can negotiate the price of a carpet in an Oriental bazaar and succeed in paying half of the requested sum just because both the seller and the buyer know that a carpet does not cost more than X or less than Y. If the seller asks ten thousand pounds for an apple or the buyer offers one pound for a car, then there will not be any bargain. But if in *Hamlet* I need a rodent that generally makes people scream, a *topo* or a mouse is enough even though I lose other properties (size, for instance, or risk of plague) that on the contrary should be preserved at any cost in Camus's context.

Accepting losses

In one of my next essays I shall deal with the problem of adapting a translation to the receiving culture. There are cases in which, talented as they are, translators are obliged to work at a loss.

In the first chapter of my last novel, *Baudolino*, I invented a pseudo-medieval North Italian language, written by a quasi-illiterate boy of Piedmontese origin, in the twelfth century, an epoch for which we do not have written Italian documents, at least not for that north-west area. My purpose was not philological exactitude; I was inspired rather by memories of the local dialect I heard in my childhood. My text can be understood in Italy even by a Southerner, who smells a sort of Northern accent (and psychology). Naturally it will be appreciated more by a Northerner who finds in it a sort of familiar slang atmosphere.

These pages created many problems for my translators. In the same period in England, Middle English existed, but it was a language which would be absolutely incomprehensible for a contemporary English speaker. And Baudolino did not live in England. To opt for a more modern dialect would have obliged Bill Weaver to choose a given Anglo-Saxon area, with the risk of making Baudolino speak, let's say, like Li'l Abner. In France there were already texts in *langue d'oc* and *langue d'oil*, and these two languages, especially the first one, were rather similar to the Northern Italian dialects. Thus Jean-Noel Schifano had the opportunity to experiment with a witty and erudite patchwork of both obsolete and still popular words and idioms. In Germany the twelfth century is the period of the Minnesänger, but even *that* German sounds very abstruse to modern German ears, and Burckhart Kroeber had to invent a balanced mixture of old and modern German. In Spain the twelfth century is the one of *El cantar de mio Cid*, and Helena Lozano found herself in the same situation as Schifano.

In all these cases it is impossible for the foreign reader to smell any original Northern Italian vernacular fragrance. In the hands of my translators the language of Baudolino became funny, full of linguistic inventions and new coinages, but it was no longer the language of a young and illiterate Piedmontese boy. And it was impossible for them to have done otherwise.

In the opening chapter Baudolino is afraid that somebody in the Imperial offices will realise that he has scratched and transformed the seminal work of the bishop Otto into a palimpsest in order to write his ungrammatical memoirs; then he cynically reflects that the court's clerks would probably not pay any attention to the loss, as they are constantly writing and rewriting a lot of useless documents. To express his scepticism Baudolino uses an obscene expression, then cancels it, deciding to use another vernacular idiom:

ma forse non li importa a nessuno in chanceleria scrivono tutto anca quando non serve et ki li trova (questi folii) si li infila nel büs de kü non se ne fa negott . . .

My Spanish translator, Helena Lozano, wanted to render Baudolino's language by an equally invented Spanish that could evoke the one of *El cantar de mio Cid* and *Fazienda de Ultramar*, an old text full of borrowed words.[1] On the other hand, confronted with this passage, she also wanted to save some original sounds, without trying to reproduce them in a medieval Spanish. Thus she tried to reproduce the original flavour of the deleted expression, simply making the vulgar word *ojete* (arsehole) a little more archaic and cutting off *kulo* by an apocope:

Pero quiçab non le importa a nadie en chancellería eschrivont tot incluso quando non sirve et kien los encuentra [isti folii] se los mete en el ollete del ku non se faz negotium . . .

Another expression used by Baudolino is *Fistiorbo che fatica skrivere mi fa già male tuti i diti.* Baudolino is simply saying that his fingers are suffering from the unusual experience of writing: *fistiorbo* is a vernacular imprecation that means 'may you become blind'. Lozano decided to Latinise this as *fistiorbus ke cansedad eskrevir.* She admits that *fistiorbus* may be incomprehensible to Spanish readers, but it was equally dull for a non-Piedmontese Italian reader.

It seems to me that analogous reflections have inspired the Catalan translator, Arenas Noguera, at least as far as the first passage is concerned:

mes potser no.l interessa negu a cancelleria scriuen tot ancar quan no
vale e qu.ils trova (ests folii) se.ls fica forat del cul no.n fa res...

For *fistiorbo* the translator simply gave a literal translation, *eu tornare orb*. Schifano made an effort to invent a French equivalent:

mais il se peut k'a nulk importe en la cancellerie ils escrivent tout
mesme quanto point ne sert et ke ki les trouve (les feuilles) kil se les
enfile dans le pertuis du kü n'en fasse goute...

Likewise, for *fistiorbo* he finds a satisfactory popular French expression, *morsoeil*. Weaver (as we shall see in a later essay) modernises and domesticates: *fistiorbo* becomes *Jesù*, which certainly functions as an expression of disappointment, but gives up any attempt to suggest the original regional atmosphere. For the first passage he employs an equally vulgar contemporary English expression (with some reticence):

but maybe nobody cares in the chancellery they write and write even
when there is no need and whoever finds them (these pages) can
shove them up his ... wont do anything about them.

The German translator, Kroeber, uses a similar method to Weaver for *fistiorbo* (which becomes a duly Germanised *verflixt swêr* – something like 'it's terribly difficult'), but does the opposite with the first passage, respecting the original expression:

aber villeicht merkets ja kainer in der kanzlei wo sie allweil irgentwas
schreiben auch wanns niëmanden nutzen tuot und wer diese bögen
findet si li infila nel büs del kü denkt sie villeicht weitewr darbei...

Even in the following chapters, where I have adopted current Italian, when Baudolino talks with his fellow citizens, vernacular expressions are frequently used. I knew that many of the subtleties would only be appreciated by readers from the same area, but I thought that readers of different regions would catch at least a certain regional flavour. Besides it is still a typical habit of Northern Italians, when they use a vernacular expression, to translate it into Italian immediately after, so as to reinforce their statement, so to speak, with the authority of a more cultivated language. So I did this in my conversations. However, this represented a challenge for my translators: if they wanted to save the double play between vernacular expressions and their immediate translation, they had to find a dialect equivalent in their own language – but in doing this they would have de-Italianised Baudolino's language. These are situations in which a loss is unavoidable.

Here is a passage from chapter 13 where I thought of the dialect idiom *squatagnè cme'n babi*, which means more or less to squash someone or something with one's foot like a toad. However, following another vernacular habit, the character was first transforming the expression into a dog-Italian, then he translated it in correct Italian:

Si, ma poi arriva il Barbarossa e vi squatagna come un babio, ovverosia vi spiaccica come un rospo.

Some translators gave up with the play on dialect-translation and used an idiom popular in their own language:

Sii, peró després arribarà Barba-roja i us esclafarà com si res.
(Noguera)

Yes, but then Barbarossa comes along and squashes you like a bug.
(Weaver)

Ja, aber dann kommt der Barbarossa und zertritt euch wie eine Kröte.
(Kroeber)

Lozano, taking advantage of the fact that the expression was immediately translated, tried a new coinage, that is, she used the original expression by adapting it to the phonetic characteristics of

Castillan. Schifano reinforced the vernacular tone of the utterance by transporting everything into a French area:

Sí, pero luego llega el Barbarroja y os escuataña como a un babio, o hablando propiamente, os revienta como a un sapo. (Lozano)

Oui, mais ensuite arrive le Barberousse et il vous réduit à une vesse de conil, autrement dit il vous souffle comme un pet de lapin. (Schifano)

It is interesting to notice that the translators who eliminated the play between vernacular and translation produced a shorter sentence than the original one.

It is impossible to analyse the various bravura pieces devised by my translators for every language, and I would rather like to deal with another phenomenon, the case of profanities and vulgar expressions. There are languages (and cultures) in which it is customary frequently to name God, the Virgin and all the saints by associating their name with vulgar expressions (usually this happens in Catholic countries like Italy and Spain); others that are pretty indulgent with curses related to sexual and scatological affairs; and others that are definitely more demure or at least extremely thrifty in mentioning Our Lord and His saints. Thus an exclamation that in Italian can sound acceptable (at most very rude but not unusual) in German would sound intolerably blasphemous. You probably remember that in Woody Allen's *Deconstructing Harry* there is a female character who repeats *fucking* every minute; well, a German lady would never do so, at least not with the same nonchalant frequency.

In the second chapter of my novel (once the vernacular introduction has ended, but popular characters still speak in a popular way) Baudolino, on his horse, enters the Church of St Sophia in Constantinople, and, to express his indignation for the simoniac behaviour of the crusaders who are pillaging the altar cloths and holy vessels, shouts some horrible profanities. The effect, at least in Italian, is intended to be grotesque because Baudolino, in order to charge the crusaders with blasphemy, utters words that Our Lord would not approve of. But to an Italian reader Baudolino appears as a scandalised (albeit excited) good Christian, and not as a follower of the Antichrist.

In Italian he says:

Ventrediddio, madonna lupa, mortediddio, schifosi bestemmiatori, maiali simoniaci, è questo il modo di trattare le cose di nostrosignore?

Bill Weaver tried to be as blasphemous as an English speaker can be, and translated this as:

God's belly! By the Virgin! 'sdeath! Filthy blasphemers, simonist pigs! Is this any way to treat the things of our lord?

Not too bad, but *Madonna lupa* defines the Virgin Mary as a she-wolf. It does not mean anything but shows a typical Catholic eagerness to deal more than informally with holy things.

Spanish, Brazilian, French and Catalan translators had no problem in rendering Baudolino's indignation:

Ventredieu, viergelouve, mordiou, répugnante sacrilèges, porcs de simoniaques, c'est la manière de traiter les choses de nostreseigneur? (Schifano)

Ventredediós, virgenloba, muertedediós, asquerosos blasfemadores, cerdos simoníacos, es ésta la manera de tratar las cosa de nuestroseñor? (Lozano)

Ventre de deus, mãe de deus, morete de deus, nojentos blasfemadores, porcos simoníacos, é este o modo de tratar las coisas de Nosso Senhor? (Lucchesi)

Pelventre dedéu, maredédeudellsops, perlamortededèu, blasfemadores fastigosos, porcos simoníacs, aquesta és manera de tractar les coses de nostre Senyor? (Arenas Noguera)

The German translator was instead extremely prudent and prudish:

Gottverfluchte Saubande, Lumpenpack, Hurenböcke, Himmelsakra, ist das die Art, wie man mit den Dingen unseres Herrn umgeht? (Kroeber)

Kroeber's Baudolino does not mention either God or the Virgin. Instead he insults the crusaders by saying that they are a herd of pigs condemned by God, a bunch of dirty rags, goats and sons of bitches, and the only pseudo-blasphemy Baudolino utters is the only one that a furious German is allowed to utter, *Himmelsakra* – that is, Heavens and Sacrament (which is not so strong, in fact). Obviously the comic effect of Baudolino's curses gets lost (since he is not uttering blasphemies in order to charge people with blasphemy) but it would have been impossible to do differently. This is another case in which the translator must accept a definite loss.

The problem of curses and four-letter words is a serious one. Once again Germans are more prudish than Spaniards, and obscenities have a different value and impact in different cultures. Here is an example from the Introduction (written in Baudolino's language) and I apologise if British ears are offended by an expression that in Northern Italy is acceptable as an example of popular talk. In this passage I was describing the way in which the city of Tortona was destroyed by the army of Frederic Barbarossa and how much the people of Pavia were excited by razing a city to the ground:

et poi vedevo i derthonesi ke usivano tutti da la Città homini donne bambini et vetuli et si plangevano adosso mentre i alamanni li portavano via come se erano beeeccie o vero berbices et universa pecora et quelli di Papìa ke alé alé entravano a Turtona come matti con fasine et martelli et masse et piconi ke a loro sbatere giù una città dai fundament li faceva sborare.

To clarify the situation, here is Weaver's translation:

And then I saw the Dhertonesi who were all coming out of the city men women and children and oldsters too and they were crying while the Alamans carried them away like they were becciee that is berbices and sheep everywhere and the people of Pavia who cheered and entered Turtona like lunnatics with faggots and hammers and clubs and picks because for them tearing down a city to the foundations was enough to make them come.

My text says that razing the city *faceva sborare* the people from Pavia, and *faceva sborare* means 'made them ejaculate' (but the popular expression is stronger than the Italian one). Weaver's translation is correct. But even an inhabitant of the Bronx might say something like this, and perhaps I preferred something more ethnic.

Jean-Noel Schifano had no hesitations in translating it into French:

> *et puis je veoie li Derthonois ki sortoient toz de la Citet homes femes enfans et vielz et ploroient en lor nombril endementre que li alemans les emmenoient com se fussent breeebies oltrement dict des berbices et universa pecora et cil de Papiia ki aIe ale entroient a Turtona com fols aveques fagots et masses et mails et pics qu 'a eulx abatre une citet jouske dedens li fondacion les faisoient deschargier les coilles ...*

Lozano employs a Latinism not for demure reasons but, as she explained to me, because the correct expression in Spanish would be *correrse*, which primarily means *to run*, and in this context everybody is moving so fast that the readers could misunderstand the expression by taking it literally, thus losing its sexual connotation:

> *et dende veia los derthonesi ke eixian todos da la Cibtat, hornini donne ninnos et vetuli de los sos oios tan fuertermientre lorando et los alamanos ge los lleuauan como si fueran beejas o sea berbices et universa ovicula et aquellotros de Papia ke arre arre entrauan en Turtona como enaxenados con faxinas et martillos et mazas et picos ca a ellos derriuar una cibtat desde los fundamenta los fazia eiaculare.*

Once again the German translator could not be too daring, and translated as:

> *und dann sah ich die Tortonesen die aus der stadt herauskamen manner .frauen kinder und greise und alle weinten und klagten indes die alemannen sie wegfürten als warens schafe und andres schlachtvieh und die aus Pavia schrien Ali Ali und stürmeten nach Tortona hinein mit äxten und hämmern und keulen und piken denn eine stadt dem erdboden gleichzumachen daz war ihnen eine grôsze lust.*

Eine grosze lust certainly evokes a sexual pleasure but is not as rude nor as immediate as *sborare*. For me, this was another radical loss, but if Kroeber had dared to use a stronger expression his readers would probably not have been convinced that Baudolino would speak in that manner.

Censorship by mutual consent

There are cases in which the loss is so unavoidable that the translator (and the author too) resign themselves to accepting a cut.

In my novels I frequently use unusual and obsolete terms and sometimes I play a game of accumulation, providing a sort of lexical *Wunderkammer*. In these situations, if, out of ten or twenty terms, one proves absolutely untranslatable, I authorise the translator to drop it: a catalogue is still a catalogue even if there are only eighteen terms instead of twenty.

Christopher Taylor[2] meticulously analysed all the cases in which Weaver, translating *Il nome della rosa*, tried to find adequate equivalents for such plant names as *viola, citiso, serpilla, giglio, ligustro, narciso, colocasia, acanto, malobatro, mirra* and *opobalsami*. It was obviously easy to find *violet, lily, narcissus, acanthus* and *myrrh*. Weaver translated *serpilla* as *thyme*: serpilla is indeed a species of thyme but Taylor remarked that *serpilla* is more rare in Italian than *thyme* in English – even though admitting that it would be 'fairly fatuous' to argue this point and that, given the horticultural differences between English and Italian, *thyme* works pretty well.

The real drama started with *citiso* and *colocasia*, for which there are no corresponding English terms. Weaver translated *citiso* as *cystus* which keeps a Latin root and a botanical flavour, and *colocasia* as *taro* which is a little more generic but, according to Taylor, correct, even though the Italian sound is more evocative. As for *opobalsami*, the English equivalent would be *balsams of Peru*, but in the Middle Ages Peru wasn't yet discovered. Weaver chose *Mecca balsam*.[3] Taylor also complains that *malobatro* became *mallow*, once again using a current term instead of an archaic one that evokes biblical psalms. But, as the author, I remember having approved those 'losses'.

In *The Name of the Rose*, in the chapter entitled 'Third Day. Sext', there are lists of rogues and lunatics wandering through various countries. The first catalogue reads:

> *Dal racconto che mi fece me lo vidi associato a quelle bande di vaganti che poi, negli anni che seguirono, sempre più vidi aggirarsi per l'Europa: falsi monaci, ciarlatani, giuntatori, arcatori, pezzenti e straccioni, lebbrosi e storpiati, ambulanti, girovaghi, cantastorie, chierici senza patria, studenti itineranti, bari, giocolieri, mercenari invalidi, giudei erranti, scampati dagli infedeli con lo spirito distrutto, folli, fuggitivi colpiti da bando, malfattori con le orecchi mozzate, sodomiti, e tra loro artigiani ambulanti, tessitori, calderai, seggiolai, arrotini, impagliatori, muratori, e ancora manigoldi di ogni risma, bari, birboni, baroni, bricconi, gaglioffi, guidoni, trucconi, calcanti, protobianti, paltonieri . . .*

And so on through a whole page. On the following page there is another list of the same kind of fellows:

> *Accapponi, lotori, protomedici, pauperes verecundi, morghigeri, affamiglioli, crociarii, alacerbati, reliquiari, affarinati, palpatori, iucchi, spectini, cochini, admirati, appezzanti e attarantanti, acconi e*

*admiracti, mutuatori, attremanti, cagnabaldi, falsibordoni, accadenti,
alacrimanti e affarfanti . . .*

It is ostentatiously erudite, perhaps, but I found all these names in
the beautiful *Il libro dei vagabondi* by Piero Camporesi,[4] and I wanted
to elicit by accumulation the vision of a crowd of tramps that
represented the primordial soup where many heretics and lumpen-
revolutionaries of that century grew up. I was charmed by the sound
of those names; I did not expect my readers to understand them but I
hoped that through the overcrowding of unusual terms they would
get the image of a situation of disorder and social fragmentation.

My translators in general rendered the first paragraph very well,
using their national repertoires and being aware that what counted
was not the absolute lexical faithfulness but rather the length and the
incongruity of the list. I quote only Weaver's translation:

From the story he told me, I pictured him among those bands of
vagrants that in the years that followed I saw more and more often
roaming about Europe: false monks, charlatans, swindlers, cheats,
tramps and tatterdemalions, lepers and cripples, jugglers, invalid
mercenaries, wandering Jews escaped from the infidels with their
spirit broken, lunatics, fugitives under banishment, malefactors with
the ears cut off, sodomites, and along with them ambulant artisans,
weavers, tinkers, chair-menders, knife-grinders, basket-weavers,
masons, and also rogues of every stripe, forgers, scoundrels,
cardsharps, rascals, bullies, reprobates, recreants, frauds, hooligans,
simoniacal . . .

As for the second list (which contained terms known only in a very
old Italian popular tradition, and that only the learned fury of
Camporesi was able to trace), the problem was more serious. Some
translators in Latin languages, like the Castilian one, translated a few
terms and for the rest adapted the Italian names to their language, as
though they were new coinages (*falsibordones, affarfantes*), or, like the
Catalan one,[5] left the Italian terms intact. It was an acceptable solution

for such similar tongues, and it was as if terms like *banderillero* or *picador* were to appear in an Italian translation from Castilian. Kroeber did a similar thing, at most Latinising some words (*falpatores, affarfantes, alacrimantes*).

Schifano found excellent equivalents in French, like *capons, rifodés, francmitous, narquois, archi-suppôts, cagous, hubins, sabouleux, farinoises, feutrards, baguenauds, trouillefous, piedebous, hapuants, attarantulés, surlacrimés, surands.* Congratulations.

The real problem came with English. A translation based upon phonetic or lexical similarity was impossible, and the Italian names would sound to an Anglo-Saxon ear like Finnish names to an Italian one. Taking into consideration that there was another list endowed with a remarkable evocative power on the previous page, we decided to cut the second one. It was certainly a loss, but we took all the risks upon ourselves.

Another unavoidable loss occurred with Adso's dream (or vision) in the chapter 'Sixth Day. Terce'. To create that dream I was largely using a medieval literary pastiche, the *Coena Cypriani*, except that I also included clips of Adso's previous experiences, bookish quotations, images from the whole repertory of the culture of those times and disjointed references to the entire history of art, languages, literature and so on. Among the innumerable quotations there was the first document of Italian language, the so-called Carta Capuana: *sao ko kelle terre per kelle fini ke ki contene, trenta anni le possette parte sancti Benedicti*, a very clear allusion for Italian readers able to remember the first chapter of their early handbook of Italian literature.

How to translate the quotation in other languages? The Castilian and Catalan versions keep it in its primitive Italian, and obviously no normal Iberian could either understand or recognise it. Schifano turned the sentence into a pseudo-ancient French (*Saü avek kes terres pour kes fins ke ki kontient*, and so on) with equally infelicitous results. He could have chosen a quotation from the *Sarment de Strasbourg*, which plays the same role as Carta Capuana in the history of French, but why would Adso have known this text? Besides, considering that

Adso was German, he would not even know the Carta Capuana – but I was obviously winking at my readers.

Kroeber had the best chance: since Adso was German, he found a quotation from the *Merseburger Zaubersprüche*, which represents the oldest document in German (*Sose benrenki, sose bluotrenki, sose lidirenki, ben zi bena, bluot zi bluoda, lid zi geliden, sose gelimida sin!*). Like me, he trusted the culture of his readers.[6]

Since Adso would not know the first document of the English language, Weaver, with my approval, decided to cut the quotation. It was, legally speaking, an act of censorship, but not a real loss since in that dream there was such an abundance of ultraviolet and malicious allusions that one more or one less did not make any difference.

Compensations

Sometimes a translator, in order not to miss an important detail, has slightly to enrich the original text. Let me turn to my experiences in translating Nerval's *Sylvie*. From now on I shall compare my solution with those of three English translators, namely Halévy (1889), Aldington (1932), and the most recent and (I think) the best one, that is, Sieburth (1995).[7]

In chapter 11 of *Sylvie* the Narrator feels embarrassment in talking with Sylvie, whom he has found transformed into a young lady so different from the innocent adolescent he knew years before. They are walking into the woods:

> *La route était déserté; j'essayais de parler des choses que j'avais dans le cœur mais, je ne sais pourquoi, je ne trouvais que des expressions vulgaires, ou bien tout à coup quelque phrase pompeuse de roman, – que Sylvie pouvait avoir lue. Je m'arrêtais alors avec un goût tout classique, et elle s'étonnait parfois de ces effusions interrompues.*

To understand the situation, let us see three English translations:

The road was deserted; I tried to speak of what was in my heart, but somehow I could find only commonplace expressions, or, occasionally, some sounding phrase from a romance, which Sylvie might have read. Then I stopped in the true classic manner, and astonished her by these broken effusions. (Halévy)

There was nobody on the road; I tried to speak to her of the thing I had in my heart; but, I do not know why, I found nothing but common expressions, or else suddenly some pompous phrases from a novel – which Sylvie might have read. (Aldington)

The road was empty; I tried to speak of what was in my heart but, I do not know why, all I could muster were vulgar commonplaces or the occasional overblown phrase from a novel – which Sylvie might well have read. I would then break off into silence in very classical fashion, leaving her somewhat bewildered by my interrupted effusions. (Sieburth)

Such *goût tout classique* has embarrassed translators, and the proof is that Aldington has ignored it. This is a typical case in which no proposition can guarantee the similarity between original and translation, since the translator feels unable to figure out what proposition the original text was expressing.

The only solution is to figure out what kind of world the original sentence pictures, and then to see what kind of sentence in the destination language can contribute to create the same world-picture in the mind of the reader. Naturally by world-picture I do not only mean a sequence of facts, but also feelings, values, psychological nuances, implicit judgements and so on. Thus I made the hypothesis that this *goût tout classique* can be understood only by referring both to the historical moment in which the story was written and published, and to the context of the chapter. Nerval fought the *bataille de l'Hernani*, that is, he took part in the Romantic movement of his time, when new forms of theatre grew up in opposition to the classical tradition of the seventeenth and eighteenth centuries; the whole chapter shows a romantic landscape scattered with the remnants of neoclassical ruins; therefore in this passage there is an opposition between the romantic emphasis and the severe tradition of the classical French theatre. Thus what Nerval suggests is that the Narrator, every time he was unable to tell what was in his heart, and feared to use literary commonplaces which Sylvie might have recognised as such, resorted to a sort of theatrical pose which recalled the solemn silences of the heroes of Corneille.

That is why I dared to add something (without, I hope, slowing the discursive rhythm) and I translated thus:

> La strada era deserta; cercai di dire quello che avevo in cuore, ma non so perché, non trovavo che espressioni banali, o al massimo qualche frase altisonante da romanzo, – che Sylvie poteva aver letto. **Allora m'irrigidivo tacendo, come un eroe da teatro classico**, ed ella si stupiva di quelle effusioni interrotte.

M'irrigidivo tacendo, come un eroe da teatro classico means, more or less, *I stiffened and was silent, like a hero of classical theatre*. I do not know whether the reader will be able clearly to see an opposition between a young Werther and a Horace rigidly and laconically reciting his *Qu'il mourût*, but I tried: I did my best to arouse in the minds of my readers the same effect that (according to my interpretation) the original text aimed at provoking in the minds of its own readers.

In chapter 3 there is an episode where a translator must not miss a shade of meaning, as it is important not only to understand the opposed psychological attitudes of the two characters who are talking to each other, but also to realise exactly what happens in the following paragraphs. The Narrator, after midnight, decides to go to Loisy (the village of his childhood, of which he has just dreamt) and approaches a *fiacre* (that is, more or less, a hansom cab) at the Palais Royal. Hearing that his customer would like him to take him eight leagues out of Paris (Sieburth translates as *twenty miles*), the driver answers (and the text says he was *moins préoccupé* than the customer), *Je vais vous conduire à la poste*. A possible translation could read *I will take you to the Post Office*, which sounds rather whimsical. Some Italian translators realised that in French *courir la poste* means to go fast, since *la poste* was at that time a station where travellers changed their horses. Thus *aller à la poste* could mean to go at full speed, to run like the wind. But, if such is the promise, why at the end of chapter 7 does Nerval write that the carriage stops on the road to Plessis and that the traveller is obliged to reach Loisy on foot – an hour's walk? Obviously the trip is not made by the private *fiacre*, which would have taken the traveller directly to Loisy.

As a matter of fact what the driver suggests is that the Narrator use a public service, and he proposes to take him to the coach station. Mail coaches also travelled at night, and at that time were the fastest service possible (twelve kilometres per hour). Certainly contemporaries of Nerval were in a position to understand *Je vais vous conduire à la poste*, but how does one make it clear to foreign readers of today? Even some modern French editions feel the necessity to put an explanatory footnote. In my translation the driver suggests taking the Narrator to the *diligenza postale*, that is, the mail coaches.

It is curious to note that while Sieburth correctly translates as *I'll drop you off at the coach station*, and so, more or less, did Halévy, Aldington translated, unreasonably, as *I'll drive you to the police station*.

Only by translating accurately can the true sense of the dialogue be expressed; the driver coldly informing his customer that a public coach will actually be faster than a private cab, shows how excited, anxious and eager to reach the village of his memories the Narrator was.

Adding and improving

It happens occasionally that, in order to avoid a possible loss, one says more than the original – and perhaps to say more means to say less, because the translator fails to keep an important and meaningful reticence or ambiguity.

In his notes to a recent Italian translation of *Moby Dick* [8] the translator, Bernardo Draghi, spends three pages apropos the famous opening line, *Call me Ishmael*. Previous Italian translators put, quite literally, *Chiamatemi Ismaele*. Draghi remarks that the original opening line suggests at least three readings: (i) 'My real name is not Ishmael, but please call me so, and try to guess what my choice means (think of the fate of Ishmael son of Abraham and Agar)'; (ii) 'My name is not important, I am only a witness of a great tragedy'; (iii) 'Let us be on first-name terms, take me as a friend, trust my report.'

Now, let us assume that Melville really wanted to suggest one or more of those readings, and that there was a reason why he did not write *My name is Ishmael* (which in Italian would be, literally, 'Mi chiamo Ismaele'). Draghi's translation reads *Diciamo che mi chiamo Ismaele*, which could be roughly translated as *Let us say that my name is Ishmael*. Even though I appreciate the rest of this translation, I cannot but object that (apart from the fact that the Italian version is less concise than the original), with his choice Draghi has inevitably stressed interpretations (i) and (ii), but has eliminated the third one. In any case he is warning the Italian reader that, in introducing the character, there is something to discover, while the English reader still remains free to decide whether or not to give particular importance to that expression. It seems to me that this translation says on one side less and on the other side more than the original. More, because it states which one of the possible readings of the original is to be selected, less because – if Melville wanted to remain ambiguous – Draghi eliminates part of the ambiguity.

Draghi's was an addition made in order to stress or to reduce the ambiguity of the source text. Sometimes, however, efforts are made at stylistic improvement. One should never try to make the source text literarily 'better'. Even bad style, clumsiness, careless repetitions must be respected. But let me now consider a borderline case in which the temptation to improve was very strong. Many years ago the publisher Einaudi started a new series of famous texts translated by writers (the same series in which I later translated *Sylvie*) and asked me to translate Dumas's *Le comte de Monte-Cristo*. I had always considered this novel a masterpiece of narrative, but to say that a given work displays a great narrative force does not mean to say that it is a literary masterpiece. Usually we appreciate books like the ones by Dumas by saying that they are works of *para-literature*. One can admit that Souvestre and Allain were not *great* writers while recognising – as happened to the Surrealists – that characters like Fantomas display a sort of mythological force.

Certainly para-literature exists, and usually we use the term to describe a lot of 'serial' stuff, dime-novels, or other kinds of books that have the one, explicit purpose of entertaining their readers, without paying attention to problems of style or of original invention. (They are successful just insofar as they are repetitive, and shamelessly respect the narrative schemes that their readers expect and ask for.) Para-literature is respectable in its own right as much as *chewing gum*, which has its own functions, even in terms of dental care, but never shows up in the menus of the *nouvelle cuisine*. However, with an author like Dumas one is entitled to ask if – in spite of the fact that he wrote for money, being paid so much per line, in order to please his public – he can be banished to para-literature.

Monte-Cristo, with its celebration of the avenger, was written because of the enormous success of Sue's *Mystères de Paris*.[9] Sue's novel aroused a sort of collective hysteria, provoking political and social reactions, and its readers identified themselves with the various characters; but if we reread it now we feel bored. On the other hand, Dumas's *The Three Musketeers* is still a pleasurable book, agile and nippy as a jazz performance. One could say then that Dumas wrote better than Sue. But such indulgent acknowledgements do not hold for *Monte-Cristo*: it was very 'badly' written.

Unbearably redundant, it shamelessly repeats the same adjectives line after line, gets bogged down with syntactically indefensible sentences, stumbles over the *consecutio temporum*, is unable to avoid sentences twenty lines long; Dumas's characters endlessly turn pale as a ghost, break into cold sweats, falter in a voice that is no longer human, and tell everybody what they have already told everybody a few pages before. It is enough to calculate how many times, in the first three chapters, Edmond tells the whole world that he is happy and wants to marry, to decide that fourteen years of prison are not enough to punish such a display of logorrhoea.

The charm of *Monte-Cristo*, then, is not due to its literary style. The problem is that literary virtues cannot only be identified by lexical elegance or syntactical fluency. They also depend on narrative rhythm, on a narrative wisdom that allows a story to transmigrate from para-literature to literature and produce mythical figures and situations which survive in the collective imagination. So it happens with many characters in fairy tales, where we usually ignore the original version and do not care how they were written – since they are equally charming even when told by one's grandmother. Fairy tales are defined as 'simple forms' as well as myths: Oedipus existed before Sophocles, Ulysses existed before Homer and the same mythical model is instantiated by the tales of the Spanish *picaros*, by Gil Blas, Simplizissimus or Till Eulenspiegel. If, then, there are simple forms, why shouldn't we accept the idea that 'simplicity' must not necessarily be identified with brevity, and that there are simple forms that are embodied in some four-hundred-or-more-page novels?

In this sense one could speak also of simple forms for works that, sometimes by chance, by carelessness and even by force of commercial speculation, contain throngs of archetypes, and produce for example cult movies like *Casablanca*.[10] *Monte-Cristo* would then belong to this category of *sludgy simple forms*, if such an oxymoron is allowed.

Let us forget for a moment questions of language and style. Let us consider only story and plot. In *Monte-Cristo* we have an incredible series of events and *coups de théâtre* that embody a series of archetypal structures that dare to define 'Christological': the innocent betrayed by his friends, a terrible descent to the hell of the Chateau d'If, the salving meeting with the Father, the Abbé Faria. It is by wrapping himself in the paternal shroud that Edmond is resurrected from the depths of the sea and starts his ascension towards an incredible power which transforms him into a Lord of the Last Judgement, who comes to absolve or condemn the living and the dead. This Avenger Christ repeatedly suffers the temptations of despair, because he is the Son of Man and is not sure of having the right to judge all sinners. Then there is the East of the Arabian Nights, the Mediterranean with its traitors and its brigands, the French society of early capitalism with all its plots and worldliness. Even though Dantès, pulled by mistake into his Bonapartist dream, does not have the complexity or the ambiguity of Julien Sorel or Fabrizio del Dongo, the fresco remains powerful. Monte-Cristo (helping the petty bourgeois and the proletarians – like him) is opposing three enemies who represent Finance, Magistrature and Army; he beats the banker by playing upon the fragility of the Stock Exchange, the magistrate by demonstrating that even judges can commit crimes, and the general by revealing a military disloyalty. Moreover, the novel offers its readers the vertigo of multiple recognitions, the fundamental spring of the old tragedy. Aristotle was satisfied with a single final revelation, while Dumas gives us a chain of uninterrupted ones. Monte-Cristo reveals himself to the world over and over again, and it is immaterial that every time the readers learn the same truth; they enjoy the astonishment of the characters and share Monte-Cristo's satisfaction even at the umpteenth revelation: they would like him never to stop proclaiming 'I am Edmond Dantès!'

However, *Monte-Cristo* is linguistically sludgy and gasping. The reasons Dumas impudently waters down his discourse are well known: he was paid so much per line and he repeats himself so often because the story was published in instalments and it was useful to remind his readers what happened before. But should we take these reasons into consideration when we translate for a modern reader? Is it not possible to do as Dumas would have done if he were paid according to the lines he saved?

I started calculating. Dumas always says that Monsieur So-and-So rises from the chair he was sitting on. That sounds boringly redundant. It would be fine to translate as *He stood up* or something similar, thus saving many words. Dumas writes:

Danglars arracha machinalement, et l'une après l'autre, les fleurs d'un magnifique oranger; quand il eut fini avec l'oranger, il s'adressa à un cactus, mais alors le cactus, d'un caractère moins facile que l'oranger, le piqua outrageusement.

It would be tolerable to translate:

> He pulled out, mechanically, the flowers of a magnificent orange tree, and when he finished he turned to a cactus that, more aggressive by nature, bit him offensively.

Such a translation makes three lines instead of four, twenty-eight English words instead of the forty-three French ones: I would have saved (and I assure you that in Italian it would be the same) more or less twenty-five per cent of the whole text. Considering that the novel, in the Pléiade edition, is 1,400 pages, I would have saved 350 pages!

This is to say nothing of the temptation to cancel all the *Monsieurs*. In French one says *monsieur* much more than in English and Italian. Even today two neighbours entering an elevator say *bonjour, monsieur,* while in English it would be enough to say *Hi* or *Good morning*. Should one translate *monsieur* every time it is uttered in a nineteenth-century novel?

I must confess that I had a crisis at this point. The presence of all those *monsieur*s not only gave the novel its French and nineteenth-century flavours, but also created conversational strategies that were essential in order to understand the mutual relationships between the various characters.

Thus I realised that all the prolixity that I had tried to avoid, as well as those 350 pages that I considered useless, had a fundamental strategic function: they contributed to create expectation, they delayed the crucial events, they were fundamental in order to stage that epiphany of revenge.

At this moment I gave up the idea of translating *Monte-Cristo*. I realised that this novel was, if not well written, at least written as it should have been, and that it couldn't be written differently. If *The Three Musketeers* had to go quickly, *Monte-Cristo* had to go slowly because it covered a lifetime of events. Dumas realised that a few pages were sufficient to recount that Jussac was defeated at a duel (because no reader would ever unsheathe a sword at the White Friars), but that many were necessary to represent a whole lifetime of frustration.

Perhaps one day I shall change my mind and try a new and pseudo translation of *Monte-Cristo*. But it will be an *adaptation* or a transmutation (see chapter 7). If I reduce the book, my readers should already know the original and accept the idea that their historical and cultural situation is different from that of Dumas's original readers. They shouldn't still be taking part in Edmond's vicissitudes, they should look at his deeds with the sceptical and ironical eye of a contemporary reader who wants only to discover how many moves Edmond had to make in order to win his game.

Effect

All the above examples tell us that the aim of a translation, more than producing any literal 'equivalence', is to create the same effect in the mind of the reader (obviously according to the translator's interpretation) as the original text wanted to create. Instead of speaking of equivalence of meaning, we can speak of *functional equivalence*: a good translation must generate the same effect aimed at by the original.[11]

Obviously this means that translators have to make an interpretative hypothesis about the effect programmed by the original text, or, to use a concept I like, to remain faithful to the *intention of the text*. Many hypotheses can be made about the intention of a text, so that the decision about what a translation should reproduce becomes *negotiable*.

Partial rewriting

Let me consider now cases in which the translator, in order to produce the same effect as intended by the original text, partially rewrites it.

A nice example of emphatic rewriting is given by the Spanish translation of *The Island of the Day Before*. I told my translators that I used a Baroque language, and often my characters indirectly quoted pieces of Italian Baroque poetry. See this passage from chapter 16 (where all the quotations I put in bold are a collage from verses of Giovan Battista Marino, the famous Italian Baroque poet):

Da quel momento la Signora fu per lui Lilia, e come Lilia le dedicava amorosi versi, che poi subito distruggeva temendo che fossero impari omaggio: **Oh dolcissima Lilia, / a pena colsi un fior, che ti perdei! / Sdegni ch'io ti riveggi? / Io ti seguo e tu fuggi, / io ti parlo e tu taci** *... Ma non le parlava se non con lo sguardo, pieno di litigioso amore, poiché più si ama e più si è inclini al rancore, provando brividi di fuoco freddo, eccitato d'egra salute, con l'animo ilare come una piuma di piombo, travolto da quei cari effetti d'amore senza affetto; e continuava a scrivere lettere che inviava senza firma alla Signora, e versi per Lilia, che tratteneva gelosamente per sé e rileggeva ogni giorno.*

Scrivendo (e non inviando), **Lilia, Lilia, ove sei? ove t'ascondi? / Lilia fulgor del cielo / venisti in un baleno / a ferire, a sparire,** *moltiplicava le sue presenze. Seguendola di notte mentre rincasava con la sua cameriera (***per le più cupe selve, / per le più cupe calli, / godrò pur di seguire, ancorché invano / del leggiadretto pié l'orme fugaci** *...), aveva scoperto dove abitava.*

Bill Weaver, in order to make English readers feel the perfume of time, has chosen a lexicon and an orthography from the seventeenth century but has translated the original verses literally. I suppose that he feared that if he resorted to examples of English euphuism he would have given his English readers a sense of exaggeration, while the verses of Marino still sound not only comprehensible but also gracious and tender to the contemporary Italian reader. In any case here is Weaver's translation, faithful enough in saying more or less what the Italian original says:

From that moment on the Lady was for him Lilia, and it was to Lilia that he dedicated amorous verses, which he then promptly destroyed, fearing they were an inadequate tribute: **Ah sweetest Lilia / hardly had I plucked a flower when I lost it! / Do you scorn** to see me? / I pursue you and you flee / I speak to you and you are mute ... But he didn't speak to her, save with his gaze full of querulous love, for the more one loves, the more one tends to rancor, shivering with cold fire, aroused by sickly health, the soul uplifted like a leaden feather, swept away by love's dear effects without affection; and he went on writing letters that he sent unsigned to the Lady, and verses for Lilia, which he jealously kept for himself, to reread them every day.

Writing (but not sending) *Lilia, Lilia, where art thou? Where dost thou hide? / Lilia, splendour of Heaven, an instant in thy presence / and I was wounded, as thou didst vanish*, he multiplied her presence. Following her at night as she returned to her house with her maid (**Through the darkest forests / along the darkest streets, / I shall enjoy following, though in vain / the fleeting prints of thy airy foot** ...), he discovered where she lived.

The Spanish translator, Helena Lozano, on the contrary, had in mind the Spanish literature of the Siglo de Oro, in many ways similar to Italian 'concettismo', but (if possible) richer in witticisms. In a commentary on her translations she notes: 'the model reader of *The Island*, and of Eco in general, is a reader who has a special taste for discovery and for whom the identification of the literary source provides an immense source of pleasure. The construction of such a reader would have been impossible without resorting to texts of the Siglo de Oro.'

She has thus decided to rewrite. In a passage which expresses, as this one does, uncontrolled ardours, what the lover said was relatively important, but the fact that he said it according to the style of his time was more relevant. 'The choice of the texts has been made taking into account the re-creative character of the translations of that time: they isolated a functional core (be it a content or a form) and developed it in their own way. In our case the relevant isotopies were the identification Lilia/flower, the loved one who escapes and her anxious pursuit. With the help of Herrera and scarcely known verses by

Góngora, and some contamination by Garcilaso, I tried to realise my purpose.'[12]

Lozano's translation thus reads:

Desde ese momento, la Señora fue para él Lilia, y como Lilia dedicábale amorosos versos, que luego destruía inmediatamente temiendo que fueran desiguales homenajes: ¡Huyendo vas Lilia de mí, / oh tú, cuyo nombre ahora / y siempre es hermosa flor / fragrantísimo esplendor / del cabello de la Aurora! ... Pero no le hablaba, sino con la mirada, lleno de litigioso amor, pues que más se ama y más se es propenso al rencor, experimentando calofríos de fuego frío excitado por flaca salud, con el ánimo jovial como pluma de plomo, arrollado por aquellos queridos efectos de amor sin afecto; y seguía escribiendo cartas que enviaba sin firma a la Señora, y versos para Lilia, que guardaba celosamente para sí y releía cada día.

Escribiendo (y no enviando) Lilia, Lilia, vida mía / ¿adónde estás? ¿A dó ascondes / de mi vista tu belleza? / ¿O por qué no, di, respondes / a la voz de mi tristeza?, multiplicaba sus presencias. Siguiéndola de noche, mientras volvía a casa con su doncella (Voy siguiendo la fuerza de mi hado / por este campo estéril y ascondido . . .), había descubierto dónde vivía.

I think that this rewriting represents an act of fidelity and that the Spanish text produces exactly the effect aimed at by the Italian original. It is true that a sophisticated reader would realise that all references are to Spanish and not Italian poetry, but the story takes place in a historical period where Northern Italy was largely under Spanish influence, and Lozano made clear that 'the condition for using that material was that it was poorly known'. Moreover, Lozano made a collage of different texts, so that it was difficult even for Spanish readers to identify the sources. They were rather invited to 'smell' a cultural climate. Which was exactly what I wanted them to do when I wrote the Italian.

There is only one objection. The Spanish version seems to mention, apropos Lilia, things, acts and features that the original

Italian text does not. To what extent should a translation be allowed to say what the original did not? We shall discuss this embarrassing question in my next chapter.

NOTES

1. Helena Lozano Miralles, 'Quando el traductor empieza a inventar: la creación léxica en la versión española de *Baudolino* de Umberto Eco', in P. Capanaga and I. Fernández García, eds., *La Neología* (Zaragoza: Pórtico, forthcoming).

2. Taylor, Christopher J., 'The Two Roses. The Original and Translated Versions of *The Name of the Rose* as Vehicles of Comparative Language Study for Translators', in Avirovič Ljljana e Dodds John, eds., Umberto Eco, Claudio Magris. *Autori e traduttori a confronto* (Trieste, 27–8 November 1989) (Udine: Campanotto, 1993), pp. 71–9.

3. Schifano (and this is the only flaw in a perfect translation), pulled by his linguistic automatism, translated *baumes du Perou*. This anachronism can be pardoned because I say in the opening pages of my novel that the manuscript that allegedly inspired me was a French nineteenth-century translation of a lost medieval text, and thus that Perou can be attributed to my pseudo-source. In fact Schifano had chosen, as a stylistic solution, not so much the imitation of a medieval chronicler but rather the style of a nineteenth-century novelist. In any case, better Mecca than Peru.

4. Torino: Einaudi, 1973.

5. *El nom de la rosa*, tr. Josep Daurell (Barcelona: Destino, 1985).

6. Obviously the meaning of the quotation is irrelevant. For the curiosity of my readers I can say that it was a magic spell suggested for medical purposes.

7. *Sylvie*, tr. Ludovic Halévy (London: Routledge, 1887); *Sylvie*, tr. Richard Aldington (London: Chatto and Windus, 1931); *Sylvie*, tr. Richard Sieburth (London: Syrens, 1995).

8. Milano: Frassinelli, 2001.

9. See my 'Rhetoric and ideology in Sue's *Les Mystères de Paris*', in *The Role of the Reader* (Bloomington: Indiana U.P., 1979).

10. See my '*Casablanca*: Cult movies and intertextual collage', in *Faith in Fakes* (London: Secker, 1986). Further edition as *Travels in Hyperreality* (London: Picador, 1987).

11. On the equivalent effect see Eugene Nida, *Towards a Science of Translation* (Leiden: Brill, 1964). For a larger discussion on these topics see Susan Bassnett-McGuire, *Translation Studies* (London/ New York: Methuen, 1980). On functional equivalence see Ian Mason, 'Communicative/functional approaches', and on *skopos* theory Christina Schäffner, '*Skopos* theory', as well as Hans Vermeer, 'Didactis of Translation', all in Mona Baker, ed., *Routledge Encyclopedia of Translation Studies* (London: Routledge, 1998). Also in this encyclopaedia see Dorothy Kenny, 'Equivalence', where several kinds of equivalence (referential, denotative, connotative, text-normative, pragmatic, dynamic, formal, functional and so on) are listed.

12. Helena Lozano Miralles, 'Comme le traducteur prit possession de l'*Ile* et commença à traduire', in Jean Petitot and Paolo Fabbri, eds., *Au nom di sens. Autour de l'oeuvre d'Umberto Eco. Colloque de Cerisy-la-Salle 1996* (Paris: Grasset, 2000).

THREE

Translation and reference

In my first essay I stated that one of the kinds of equivalence that could be judged as essential for a translation was *referential equivalence*. In very simple terms, a translation should convey the same things and events as the original.

I mean reference in its strictest sense,[1] that is, an act by which, once one knows the meaning of the uttered words, one determines states of a possible world (which can be either the world we are living in or the one described by a novel), and asserts that in a given spatio-temporal situation certain things or certain events happen. As Strawson said, 'mentioning or referring is not something an expression does; it is something that someone can use an expression to do'.[2] *Cats are mammals* is not, from my point of view, an act of referring, because it simply establishes which properties we should assign to cats in general in order to use, in the course of a verbal interaction, the word *cat*. The same would happen with the phrase *unicorns are white*. In Strawson's terms, 'to give the meaning of an expression . . . is to give *general directions* for its use to refer to or to mention particular objects and persons; to give the meaning of a sentence is to give *general directions* for its use in making true or false assertions'. If somebody says that *cats are amphibians* or *unicorns have a striped mantle*, one should not say that these two assertions are 'false', but more properly that they are 'wrong', at least if we follow zoology manuals and all the traditional descriptions of unicorns found in ancient bestiaries. In order to decide that *cats are amphibians* is a correct assertion I would have to ask the whole of society to restructure its entire system of natural classifications, as happened when the learned community decided to consider the assertion *dolphins are fishes* as wrong.

On the other hand expressions like *there is a cat on the mat, my cat Felix is sick* or *Marco Polo said to have seen unicorns* are referring to situations of the actual world (including the fact that Marco Polo reported having seen unicorns). These assertions can be empirically tested and judged as true or false. In ordinary situations we react to *cats are mammals* and *there is a cat on the mat* in two different ways. In the first case we open an encyclopaedia in order to see if the statement is correct; in the second, if we do not trust the speaker, we check *de visu*, to ascertain whether the statement is true.

Now, most of the texts people translate are reports on facts, narrations, poems and so on, and all of them mention something that should be taken as if it were the case. A newspaper article saying that so and so died yesterday presupposes that we take for granted that so-and-so is really dead. A novel saying that Prince Andrei died commits the readers to take for granted that (in the possible world of that novel) Prince Andrei really died – to such an extent that, if the narrator shows him alive and well in the course of the novel, the reader will feel astonished. In the same vein they will consider the assertion of another character, who says that Andrei is still living, a lie.

A novel describes a world (a possible one, even though not necessarily a fictitious one, as in historical novels). Translators are not allowed to change the true references to that world and no translator could say, in his version, that David Copperfield lived in Madrid or Don Quixote in Devonshire.

Such restrictions admit many exceptions. For instance, when a given expression has a connotative force it must keep the same force in translation, even at the cost of accepting changes in denotation. To make a very elementary example, if an English text says that *it is raining cats and dogs*, no Italian translator is obliged to respect the reference and to translate as *piove cani e gatti* because the expression does not mean anything in Italian. In Italian one would say *piove come dio la manda*.

Thus a provocative question can be: to what extent, in order to preserve its proper effect, can a text be altered without violating the equivalence in reference?

Disregarding reference

In my translation of *Sylvie*, an instance in which I felt obliged to make a modification in terms of reference was that of the visit to Châalis in chapter 7. Nerval says that it takes place *le soir de la Saint-Barthélemy* and a little further on he speaks of *le jour de la Saint-Barthélemy*. There is no contradiction because the evening of St Bartholomew belongs to St Bartholomew's day. Translators usually faithfully render *the evening* in the first occurrence, and *the day* in the second. Now, for every French reader it is enough to mention *la Saint-Barthélemy* to evoke the night of one of the most cruel massacres of European history, but in Italian the same connotation is provided by the expression 'la notte di san Bartolomeo'; the *night* of St Bartholomew – not the evening or the day, but the night. Since the whole scene undoubtedly takes place in the dark, I disregarded both *soir* and *jour* and translated as *notte*, night, in both cases, without betraying the intentions of the text and at the same time giving my readers the right suggestion.

I decided that it was contextually relevant that the event took place during the night, while the original text stated that it was taking place during the evening. It is certainly difficult to tell the difference between night and evening, especially considering that at the time of *Sylvie* people in the countryside went to bed very early, so that what for us is still early evening for them was probably deep night. In any case I have taken a decision that violates the 'referential duty' of the translator. Let me elaborate a little more on this point.

In my book *The Role of the Reader* I analysed a short story by Alphonse Allais, *Un drame bien parisien*, and my friend Fredric Jameson translated it into English for me in the 1970s. In the second chapter the two protagonists Raoul and Marguerite, coming back from the theatre, return home in a *coupé*, and start quarrelling. Note that this quarrel is rather relevant for the further course of the story.

Jameson's translation says that they returned home in a hansom cab. Is *hansom cab* a good translation for *coupé*? Dictionaries say that a coupé is a 'short four-wheeled closed carriage with an inside seat for two and an outside seat on the front for the driver'. As such a coupé is frequently confused with a brougham but broughams may have two or four wheels and two or four places, and undoubtedly have their driver's seat *at the rear*. A hansom cab is more or less similar to a brougham: it has two wheels, it is closed and has the driver's seat *behind*. Thus when one compares a coupé with a hansom, the position of the driver's seat becomes *diagnostic*, just as the statement 'single place for sitting' is diagnostic, even indispensable, in order to tell the difference between an armchair and a sofa. A diagnostic difference could become crucial in certain contexts. Was it crucial in *Un drame*, and was Jameson's translation an unfaithful one?

I do not know why Jameson did not use the word *coupé*, which is admitted by the English dictionary. Probably he thought that *hansom* was more comprehensible than *coupé* for the average English reader, especially as coupé today means a kind of motor car. If so, his choice was a convenient case of negotiation.

The translator ought at least to make evident that the two protagonists are going home in a horse-drawn vehicle, but the fact that they are quarrelling is particularly relevant, as is the fact that they, being a decent bourgeois couple, must solve their problems *privately*. What they needed was a *closed bourgeois private* carriage, not a popular omnibus. In such a situation the position of the driver's seat is irrelevant. A coupé, a brougham or a hansom would have been equally good. As it was not essential for the reader to know the position of the driver, it could have been neglected.

However, the original text said that Raoul and Marguerite went home in a coupé and the translation says that they used a different kind of carriage. Let us try to visualise the scene. In the French text the couple travel in a carriage with the driver sitting in front; in the English version a competent reader would know that the driver was sitting behind. I have just said that, in this context, the difference is irrelevant, but from the point of view of a truth-conditional semantics the two texts stage two different scenes, or two different possible worlds where two individuals are in a different situation. If a newspaper said the Prime Minister arrived at the site of a disaster by helicopter, while in fact he arrived by car, many readers would find the difference relevant: was or was not the Prime Minister solicitous regarding the tragic event?

In my *Foucault's Pendulum* the three protagonists (Casaubon, Belbo and Diotallevi) frequently indulge in literary quotations and seem incapable of seeing the world except through their literary recollections. In chapter 57 there is a description of a drive in the hills, and Casaubon reports:

> . . . *man mano che procedevamo, l'orizzonte si faceva vasto, benché a ogni curva aumentassero i picchi, su cui si arroccava qualche villaggio. Ma tra picco e picco si aprivano orizzonti interminati – al di là della siepe, come osservava Diotallevi . . .*

This passage says that the characters drive through the hills and see beautiful landscapes, so that they have the impression of glimpsing boundless horizons *al di là della siepe*, which should be correctly and literally translated as *beyond the hedge*. Since that hedge is presented as *the* hedge, the reader might feel confused because no hedge was previously mentioned. However, I was sure that every Italian reader (in any case every reader interested in my novel) would recognise that hedge, which canonically comes from the intertextual milieu of Italian literature: the *siepe*, the hedge, is the one mentioned by Giacomo Leopardi in his *L'infinito*, perhap the most famous poem of Italian Romanticism, whose translation reads:

> I always loved this solitary hill,
> This hedge as well, which takes so large a share
> Of the far-flung horizon from my view;

But seated here, in contemplation lost,
My thought discovers vaster space beyond
Supernal silence and unfathomed peace.

The Italian reader would understand that Diotallevi can enjoy the landscape only through the poetical experience of somebody else.

I told my various translators that neither the hedge nor the allusion to Leopardi were important but I insisted that a literary clue should be kept at all costs. I told them that the presence of a castle or a tree instead of a hedge made no difference to me, provided that the castle and the tree evoked a famous passage in their own national literature, in the context of the description of a magical landscape. This is how some translators solved the problem:

> *Mas entre un pic et l'autre s'ouvraient des horizons infinis-au dessus des étangs, au-dessus des vallées, comme observait Diotallevi . . .* (Schifano)

> *Doch zwischen den Gipfeln taten sich endlose Horizon te auf-ienseits des Heckenzaunes, wie Diotallevi bemerkte . . .* (Kroeber)

> *Pero entre pico y pico se abrían horizontes ilimitados: el sublime espacioso llano, como observaba Diotallevi . . .* (Pochtar/Lozano)

> *Però entre pic i pic s'obrien horizonts interminables: tot era prop i lluny, i tot tenia com un resplendor d'eternitat, com ho observava Diotallevi . . .* (Vicens)

Weaver simply translated, with an explicit reference to Keats, as:

> . . . at every curve the peaks grew, some crowned by little villages; we glimpsed endless vista. Like Darién, Diotallevi remarked . . . (Weaver)

Similar solutions were adopted in analogous cases. In chapter 29 Casaubon says that:

La sera era dolce ma, come avrebbe scritto Belbo nei suoi files, esausto di letteratura, non spirava un alito di vento.

I reminded my translators that *non spirava un alito di vento* was a recognisable quotation from Manzoni's *The Betrothed*, and that, as in the case of the hedge, they should find a recognisable literary quotation in their language. Some of the solutions follow:

It was a mild evening; as Belbo, exhausted with literature, might have put in one of his files, there was naught but a lovely sighing of the wind. (Weaver)

Le soir était doux mais, comme l'aurait écrit Belbo dans ses files, harassé de littérature, les souffles de la nuit ne flottaient pas sur Galgala. (Schifano)

Es war ein schöner Abend, aber, wie Belbo bekifft von Literatur in seinen files geschrieben hätte, kein Lufthauch regte sich, über alle Gipfeln war Ruh. (Kroeber)

I particularly like Kroeber's solution: *Kein Lufthauch regte sich* means more or less that there was no wind, but *uber alle Gipfeln war Ruh* means *on the top of the mountains there was silence* – a beautiful quotation from Goethe. By adding those mountains which really have nothing to do with the context (the scene takes place in a hotel room at Bahia in Brazil) the 'literariness' of the remark becomes more blatant.

Let me quote another example from *The Island of the Day Before*. As I have said, this novel is essentially a parody of the Baroque style and includes many implicit quotations from poets and writers of the time. In chapter 32 Roberto de la Grive describes the coral in the Pacific Ocean as he saw it for the first time in his life. He could only use metaphors and similes based on plants and minerals he knew. The most vivid impression Roberto receives from the coral is that of a wide variety of colours and of several shades of the same colour. In fact this is the main impression everybody feels when seeing coral in the Southern Seas. My problem was to express such a visual variety verbally. My goal was to create, through a plurality of colour terms, the visual impression of a plurality of colours. Thus I employed all the colour terms provided by the Italian lexicon, including obsolete words from seventeenth-century literature. My stylistic purpose was obviously 'never to use the same term twice'.

My translators were supposed to create the same linguistic effect in their own language, but I suspected that different languages might have different numbers of terms for the same colour.

For instance, Lozano faced a similar problem when trying to translate from chapter 22, where Father Caspar describes the mysterious Orange Dove and, since he is incapable of finding adequate colour terms to express the delicate shades of red of its plumage, Roberto suggests:

> *Rubbio, rubeo, rossetto, rubeolo, rubescente, rubecchio, rossino, rubefacente, suggeriva Roberto.* Nein, Nein, *si irritava padre Caspar. E Roberto: come una fragola, un geranio, un lampone, una marasca, un ravanello . . .*

Weaver's translation reads:

> Ruddy, ruby, rubescent, rubedinous, rubent, rubefacient, Roberto suggested. *Nein, nein,* Father Caspar became irritated. Roberto went on: like a strawberry, a geranium, a raspberry, a cherry, a radish . . .

When checking Weaver's translation I did not realise that he was quoting only six English colour terms instead of my eight Italian terms. Probably he could not find more words for red and thought that six were enough to suggest the impatience of Roberto. Lozano too had to surrender because, as she says,[3] in Spanish she only found six terms. Moreover in Spain in the seventeenth century a geranium was called a *pico de cigüeña* (crane bill) and – beyond the fact that this term is now obsolete and incomprehensible to modern readers – its use risked introducing an 'animal' element into a 'vegetal' series. Thus she substituted the geranium with another flower, equally red:

Rojo, rubro, rubicundo, rubio, rufo, rojeante, rosicler, sugería Roberto. Nein, nein, irritábase el padre Caspar. Y Roberto: como una fresa, una clavellina, una frambuesa, una guinda, un rabanillo . . .

Let me praise Schifano for having found eight terms: *rouille, rougeâtre, rubis, rubicund, rougeaud, roussâtre, rocou, rubéfié.*

To come back to coral, and featuring that in a given language there weren't, let's say, enough terms for yellow, I encouraged my translators to change colours freely when they ran out of words. In those seas, coral and fish come in all colours, and that a given coral or fish was red or yellow was not important; I repeat, what counted was that the same term would not be repeated in the same context and that the reader, like Roberto, experienced a great chromatic variety through a linguistic variety.

So when I said that *si vedeva il fegato poroso color colchico di un grande animale* (that is, in my translation, *there was a sort of porous liver the colour of an autumn crocus*) I left the colour undetermined, since crocus petals may be yellow, lilac or whatever. Weaver chose *saffron*, Kroeber *lilarote*.

When I speak of *polipi soriani* (where *soriani* evokes the striped coat of a tabby cat), Weaver speaks of *cypress-polyps*, Lozano of *polipos sirios*, and Schifano of *polypes ocellés* (ocellated). The German translator found a more literal solution by speaking of *getigerte Polypen*. But when, a little later, I speak of *tuberi tigrati di ramature negricanti*, and the translators used *striped tubers*, *tubercules tigrés* and *raigones listado*, Kroeber, having already called the polyps *getigerte*, was then obliged to change both form and colour for my tubers, speaking of *gelblich geflammete Knollen schwärzlichen Astwerks*, that is, more or less, of black branches, which show yellow protuberances.

In all these examples I invited the translators to disregard the literal sense of my text in order to preserve what I considered to be the 'deep' one, or the effect it had to produce.

Would we say that my translators (with my approval) have changed my text? We certainly would. In spite of this, these translations say exactly what I wanted to say, that is, that my three characters were sick of literature, and that the coral of the Southern Seas is incredibly marvellous – and a literal translation would have made these effects less perspicuous.

However, we must admit that these translations are *referentially false*.

Thus, to preserve the effect of the text, translators were entitled not only to make radical changes to the literal meaning of the original text, but also to its reference – since in Italian Diotallevi is said to have seen a hedge, Casaubon to have said *non spirava un alito di vento*, Roberto to have seen such and such colours and forms, while in other languages this is not the case. Can a translation preserve the sense of a text by changing its reference?

No one would allow a French translator of *Hamlet* to write, for instance, that Hamlet, instead of seeing the ghost of his father, saw the ghost of somebody else. Obviously, one could say that Shakespeare cannot be changed, not even to help his foreign readers to understand certain situations, while Eco's translators can do what they want. But we have seen that it is not so wrong, in an Italian translation of *Hamlet*, to mention a *topo* (that is, a *mouse*) instead of a *rat*. Yet such a variation becomes highly relevant, as we have seen, in a translation of Camus's *La peste*.

Surface and deep stories

If, in order to preserve the deep sense of a text, a translation can change its references, to what extent are these changes possible? We have to reconsider the distinction between story and plot I mentioned in my first essay, as well as the nature of the reading process, by which every sentence or sequence of sentences conveying a story can be summarised (or interpreted) by a micro-proposition and several micro-propositions can be summarised by a more comprehensive macro-proposition.

Which were the 'real' stories told by the pages of my novels? The fact that Diotallevi saw a hedge or the fact that he was a sort of culture snob, able to perceive nature only if filtered through poetry? The fact that Roberto saw striped tubers instead of black branches with yellow protuberances, or the fact that he was amazed by an inexhaustible quantity of colours and forms and realised he was (as the title of the chapter suggests) in a Garden of Delights?

In order to make the 'deep' story of a chapter or of an entire novel detectable, translators are entitled to change several 'surface' stories.

For instance, the page on coral from *The Island of the Day Before* can be summarised as:

1. Roberto is swimming on the coral reef.
He admires an immense variety of forms and colours.

These micro-propositions can be embedded in larger macro-propositions and the whole chapter could be summarised as:

2. Thinking that his brother is on the island, Roberto decides to learn how to swim.
In the course of his efforts, day by day, he discovers the marvels of the coral reef.
Among the coral he finds a sort of mineral form that he picks up as thinking it is the skull of Father Caspar.

The whole novel could be summarised by a hyper-macro-proposition that reads:

3. Roberto is shipwrecked on an abandoned boat near an island.
He is west of the 180° meridian, the island is east.
He will never reach it, and thus he fails to live in the day before.

Given that stories are embedded in this way, to what extent are translators entitled to change a surface story in order to preserve a deep one?

It is clear that every single text permits a different and individual solution. Common sense suggests that translators can change *Roberto saw a striped polyp* into *Roberto saw an ocellated polyp* but they certainly are not allowed to change the global macro-proposition (3) by writing, let us say, that Roberto reaches the island.

A first hypothesis is that one can change the literal meaning of single sentences in order to preserve the sense of the corresponding micro-propositions, but cannot alter the sense of major macro-propositions. But what about the many intermediate 'shallow' stories (between the literal meaning of single sentences and the global sense of an entire novel)? What if a translator decides to change a joke, or a play on words impossible to translate, by assuming that the sense of the story is not that a character told *that* joke but that he or she told *a* joke?

It is on the basis of interpretative decisions of this kind that translators play the game of faithfulness.

Radical rewriting

In my last essay I considered cases in which a *partial* rewriting (like the substitution of Baroque verses in Lozano's translation) aimed at keeping the general textual effect. Let me now consider cases in which, in order to compensate for a loss, the operation of rewriting substantially alters the reference of the original text – which is profoundly transformed, disregarding the matter of semantic equivalence, in order to play the same game with the target text that the author played with the source text.

A typical case of *radical* rewriting is the Italian translation of James Joyce's 'Anna Livia Plurabelle', part of *Finnegans Wake*. This translation originally appeared under the names of Nino Frank and Ettore Settanni (who certainly contributed to the work) but must be considered as the work of Joyce himself,[4] as was the French translation, which was made by Joyce in collaboration with Beckett, Soupault, and others.[5]

Finnegans Wake is written in 'Finneganian', which could be defined as an invented language. As a matter of fact it is a multilingual text, but a multilingual text written by an English-speaker. Thus Joyce's decision was based on the idea that the Italian and the French versions had to be multilingual texts written by an Italian or a French speaker.

We shall see in my next essay that Humboldt suggests that translating means not only leading the reader to understand the language and culture of the original but also enriching one's own language. We can thus say that for Joyce the Italian and French translations of *Finnegans Wake* were conceived in order to lead the French and Italians to express what they were unable to express before (just as Joyce did with English).

Here is an example of rewriting that pushes the limits of the original creation:

> Tell us in franca lingua. And call a spate a spate. Did they never sharee you ebro at skol, you antiabecedarian? It's just the same as if I was to go par examplum now in conservancy's cause out of telekinesis and proxenete you. For coxyt sake and is that what she is?

First of all we have to remember that in the episode of Anna Livia Joyce succeeded in mentioning eight hundred rivers (frequently concealing their names with a pun). This happens also in these lines: *call a spate a spate* suggests the colloquial invitation to talk plainly without any frills but also implies a fluvial connotation, in this case a flood of speech. *Sharee* unites *share* and the river Shari, *ebro* unites *Hebrew* and the Ebro, *skol* unites *school* and the river Skollis. To skip other references, like the one to the early Christian antiabecedarian heresy, *for coxyt sake* brings to mind the infernal river Cocytus and the Cox River as well as *for God's sake* (and therefore an invocation, in this context, that is blasphemous).

Here we have three translations, the French one, Joyce's Italian version and the most recent Italian one by Luigi Schenoni:[6]

Pousse le en franca lingua. Et appelle une crue une crue. Ne t'a-t-on pas instruit l'ébreu à l'escaule, espèce d'antibabébibobu? C'est tout pareil comme si par example je te prends subite par telekinesis et te proxénetise. Nom de flieuve, voilà ce qu'elle est? (French)

Dillo in lingua franca. E chiama piena piena. T'hanno mai imparato l'ebro all'iscuola, antebecedariana che sei? E' proprio siccome circassi io a mal d'esempio da tamigiaturgia di prossenetarti a te. Ostrigotta, ora capesco. (Italian)

Diccelo in franca lingua. E dì piena alla piena. Non ti hanno mai fatto sharivedere un ebro a skola, pezzo di antialfabetica. E' proprio come se ora io adassi par exemplum fino alla commissione di controllo del porto e ti prossenetizzassi. Per amor del cogito, di questo si tratta? (Schenoni's Italian)

I feel unable to identify all the allusions of the French text and I only remark that it tries to save some names of rivers and solves the last invocation with an allusion to blasphemy, where *nom de flieuve* evokes *nom de dieu*.

Schenoni, in order to express the play on words in *call a spate a spate*, follows the previous Joycean translation. *To call a spade a spade* is regularly translated in Italian as *dire pane al pane* (call bread bread): thus *piena* evokes *pane* and also correctly translates *flood* (and thus also *spate*). At the same time Schenoni recuperates some rivers that the original text mentions two pages later, namely, Pian Creek, Piana and Pienaars. He also saves the river Shari (Joyce loses it), along with Ebro and Skol, but misses the theological allusion of antiabecedarian, takes *conservancy* rather literally as 'a commission authorised to supervise a forest, river or port', and keeps Cocytus – with a witty reference to Descartes's *cogito* but abandoning every blasphemous connotation.

Now, let's see what Joyce did. Faced with the difficulty of

rendering the allusions of the original, especially in the second part, he gives up with the original text (his own!) and tries unheard-of allusions, such as that Italian subjunctive *cercassi* (if I tried) which becomes *circassi*, and thus suggest *circassian*, and decides to recuperate (via thaumaturgy instead of telekinesis) another river mentioned elsewhere, the Thames (*Tamigi* in Italian). But this is not enough for Joyce as a re-creating translator. He is aware that the deep meaning of the passage, over and beyond the play of quotation and reference, is that of a perplexed and diabolic uncertainty in the face of the mysteries of a *lingua franca* that, like *Finnegans Wake*, derives from different languages and looks like a Babel-like disaster, a barbarian pidgin. Thus, after having evoked barbarians with *circassian*, Joyce does something more: he introduces as a closing phrase something that did not exist in English, that is, *Ostrigotta, ora capesco*.

Ostrigotta is a pun made by *ostregheta* (a prudent Venetian correction for the blasphemy *ostia!* – literally, *by the host!*), by *ostrogoto*, Ostrogothic, as a suggestion of incomprehensible barbarian languages (let's remember that *Finnegans Wake* at one point defines itself as an *Ostrogothic kakography*), and *Gott* (God). Blasphemy uttered about an incomprehensible tongue. It would be natural to end with *non capisco* (I do not understand). But *ostrigotta* also suggests *I got it*, and Joyce writes *ora capesco*, which is a pun on *capisco* (I understand) and *esco* (I get out): Joyce gets out from his own linguistic labyrinth of the Finneganian *meandertale*.

Compared with the original, Joyce's Italian translation says completely different things. Joyce, in rewriting his own text, felt the need to invent an expression like *Ostrigotta, ora capesco*. The real deep sense of *Finnegans Wake* for him was to show the possibilities of a language. In order to elicit such an effect, he did not care about problems of reference. He was sure of making a good translation of his own source text by saying something different.

This is not an example to hold up in a translators' school, and I would not propose it as a paramount case of fair negotiation. It shows, however, to what extent the principle of equal reference can be violated for the sake of a *deeply* equivalent translation.

Another case of rewriting is instanced by my translation of the *Exercices de style* by Queneau, where I was frequently obliged not to translate, but rather (once I understood what kind of word game the author was playing), to try playing the same game, following the same rules, in another language.

The exercises started from a basic text:

Dans l'S, à une heure d'affluence. Un type dans les vingt-six ans, chapeau mou avec cordon remplaçant le ruban, cou trop long comme si on lui avait tiré dessus. Les gens descendent. Le type en question s'irrite contre un voison. Il lui reproche de le bousculer chaque fois qu'il passe quelqu'un. Ton pleurnichard qui se veut méchant. Comme il voit une place libre, se précipite dessus.

Deux heures plus tard, je le rencontre Cour de Rome, devant la gare Saint-Lazare. Il est avec un camarade qui lui dit: 'Tu devrais faire mettre un bouton supplémentaire à ton pardessus.' Il lui montre où (à l'échancrure) et pourquoi.

On the line S bus, at rush hour. A guy about twenty-six years old, wearing a soft hat with a cord instead of a ribbon, too long a neck, as though somebody had pulled it. People get off. The guy gets annoyed with a fellow passenger. Complains that he's pushing him every time someone goes by. A wimp who wants to be a tough guy. As soon as he sees a free seat, he makes a dive for it.

Two hours later, I see him again at the Cour de Rome, outside the Gare Saint-Lazare. He's with a friend who's telling him: 'You ought to get an extra button put on your coat.' He explains where (near the lapels) and why.[7]

That's all. But Queneau succeeds in retelling the same story through a hundred variations on the same theme.

Some exercises are clearly concerned with content (the basic text is modified by litotes, in the form of a prediction, a dream, a press release, etc.) and can be translated more or less literally. Others are concerned with expression (there are word games of anagrams, permutations by an increasing number of letters, lipograms, onomato-poeia, syncope, metathesis), etc. There was nothing else for it but to rewrite.

Queneau's exercises also include references to poetic forms: where the original text told the story in alexandrines, for example, in parodistic reference to the French literary tradition, I took the liberty of telling the same story with an equally parodistic reference to one of Leopardi's cantos. In one variation the French text was using pseudo-Anglicisms:

Un dai vers middai, je tèque le beusse et je sie un jeugne manne avec une grète nèque et un hatte avec une quainnde de lèsse tresses. Soudainement ce jeugne manne bi-queumze crézé et acquiouse un respectable seur de lui trider sur les toses. Puis il reunna vers un site eunoccupé.

    A une lète aoure je le sie égaine; il vouoquait eupe et daoune devant le Ceinte Lazare stécheunne. Un beau lui guivait un advice à propos de beutone.

To translate French Anglicisms into Italian Anglicisms is not so difficult, provided one does not translate literally but rather tries to imagine how an Italian would speak in garbled English:

Un dèi, veso middèi, ho takato il bus and ho seen un yungo manno co uno greit necco e un hatto con una ropa texturata. Molto quicko questo yungo manno becoma crazo e acchiusa un molto respettabile sir di smashargli i fitti. Den quello runna tovardo un anocchiupato sitto.

    Leiter lo vedo againo che ualcava alla steiscione Seintlàsar con uno friendo che gli ghiva suggestioni sopro un bàtton del cot.

Another exercise was entitled *Italianismes*, that is, it was written in a sort of garbled French in Italian style:

Oune giorne en pleiné merigge, ié saille sulla plata-forme d'oune otobousse et là quel ouome ié vidis? ié vidis oune djiovanouome au

longué col avé de la treccie otour du cappel. Et le dittò djiovanouome
au longuer col avé de la treccie outour du cappel. Et lé ditto
djiovaneouome aoltragge ouno pouovre ouome à qui il rimproveravait
de lui pester les pieds et il ne lui pestarait noullément les pieds, mai
quand il vidit oune sedie vouote, il corrit por sedersi là.

One cannot translate dog-Italian into dog-Italian and I was obliged
to shift to an Italian drenched with Gallicisms. This was the result:

Allora, und jorno verso mesojorno egli mi è arrivato di rencontrare su
la bagnola de la linea Es un signor molto marante con un cappello
tutt'affatto extraordinario, enturato da una fisella in luogo del rubano
et un collo molto elongato. Questo signor là si è messo a discutar con
un altro signor che gli pietinava sui piedi expresso; e minacciava di lui
cassare la figura. Di' dunque! Tutto a colpo questo mecco va a seder su
una piazza libera.

The cases of Joyce and Queneau raise another problem, concerning the adaptation of a text, born in a given cultural milieu, to the
spirit and possibilities of comprehension of readers belonging to
another culture.

NOTES

1. See chapter 6 in my *Kant and the Platypus* (New York: Harcourt/
   London: Secker, 1999).
2. Peter Strawson, 'On referring', *Mind* lix (1950).
3. Helena Lozano Miralles, 'Comme le traducteur prit possession de
   l'*Ile* et commença à traduire', in Jean Petitot and Paolo Fabbri, eds.
   *Au nom di sens. Autour de l'oeuvre d'Umberto Eco. Colloque de
   Cerisy-la-Salle 1996* (Paris: Grasset, 2000).
4. 'Anna Livia Plurabella', *Prospettive* iv, 2, 11–12 (1940). This version
   contained interpolations by Ettore Settanni. A first version, which
   sprang from the collaboration between Joyce and Nino Frank,
   dated 1938, was edited by Jacqueline Risset in Joyce, *Scritti italiani*

(Milano: Mondadori, 1979). The Italian version, the French one, the original text and other subsequent versions are now in Joyce, *Anna Livia Plurabelle*, edited by Rosa Maria Bollettieri Bosinelli (Turin: Einaudi 1996), with my introduction.

5. 'Anna Livia Plurabelle', *La Nouvelle Revue Française* xix, 212 (1931). Even though the French translation was from the 1928 version of 'Anna Livia' and the Italian one from the final 1939 version, there are no important variations regarding the points I shall mention.
6. *Finnegans Wake*, tr. Luigi Schenoni (Milano: Mondadori, 2001), p. 198 bis.
7. Raymond Queneau, *Exercises in Style*, tr. Barbara Wright (New York: New Directions, 1981).

FOUR

Source vs target

In his essay on 'The misery and splendor of translation', Ortega y Gasset says that, contrary to Meillet's opinion, it is not true that every language can express everything (as mentioned, Quine[1] said that in a jungle language one cannot translate the phrase *neutrinos lack mass*). According to Ortega:

> The Basque language ... forgot to include in its vocabulary a term to designate God and it was necessary to pick a phrase that meant 'lord over the heights' – *Jaungoikua*. Since lordly authority disappeared centuries ago, *Jaungoikua* today directly means God, but we must place ourselves in the time when one was obliged to think of God as a political, worldly authority, to think of God as a civil governor or similar. To be exact, this case reveals to us that lacking a name for God made it very difficult for the Basques to think about God. For that reason they were very slow in being converted to Christianity.[2]

I always feel sceptical about this sort of naive Sapir-Whorf hypothesis. According to Ortega's argument, English-speakers should have an incorrect idea of God since they also call him Lord. Schleiermacher in his *On the Different Methods of Translating*[3] remarked that, obviously, 'all humans are under the sway of the language they speak; they and their entire thinking are a product of that language, so that it is impossible to think with a complete clarity anything that lies beyond its boundaries.' But a few lines later he added: 'On the other hand, all free-thinking people with any mental initiative at all also play their part in shaping their language.' Humboldt[4] was the first to speak about the way in which translations can 'augment the significance and expressivity of the native language'.

In spite of such a confidence in the dynamic capacity of languages to evolve when exposed to a foreign challenge, we still have some difficulty in deciding if the *Elohim* who shows (or show) up at the beginning of the Bible can be truly translated as God.

Understanding Dante

As has been said, translation is always a shift, not between two languages but between two cultures – or two encyclopaedias. A translator must take into account rules that are not strictly linguistic but, broadly speaking, cultural.

As a matter of fact the same happens when we read a text which is centuries old. Steiner, in the first chapter of his *After Babel*,[5] shows very well how certain texts of Shakespeare and Jane Austen are not fully comprehensible to a contemporary English reader who does not have an understanding of the vocabulary and the cultural background of their authors.

Starting from the principle that Italian, in the course of the last seven centuries, changed less than other European languages, every Italian student is convinced they perfectly understand this famous sonnet by Dante:

> *Tanto **gentile** e tanto **onesta pare***
> *la **donna** mia, quand'ella altrui saluta,*
> *ch'ogne lingua deven tremando muta,*
> *e li occhi no l'ardiscon di guardare.*
> *Ella si va, sentendosi laudare,*
> ***benignamente** d'**umiltà** vestuta;*
> *e par che sia una **cosa** venuta*
> *da cielo in terra a **miracol** mostrare.*

The common way of understanding these lines could be rendered in English as 'My woman, when she greets a passer-by, looks so courteous [or polite] and so honest that every tongue can only babble and our eyes do not dare to look at her. She walks hearing people praising her, benignly and dressed in all humility, and truly seems a thing come from the skies to show a miracle on earth.'

There are three English translations. The first is from a Pre-Raphaelite author, Dante Gabriel Rossetti:[6]

My lady looks so gentle and so pure
When yielding salutation by the way,
That the tongue trembles and has nought to say,
And the eyes, which fain would see, may not endure.
And still, amid the praise she hears secure,
She walks with humbleness for her array;
Seeming a creature sent from Heaven to stay
On earth, and show a miracle made sure.

A contemporary translator, Mark Musa,[8] reads:

Such sweet decorum and such gentle grace
attend my lady's greetings as she moves
that lips can only tremble in silence
and eyes dare not attempt to gaze at her.
Moving, benignly clothed in humility,
untouched by all the praise along her way,
she seems to be a creature come from Heaven
to earth, to manifest a miracle.

Marion Shores translates:[8]

My lady seems so fine and full of grace
When she greets others, passing on her way,
That trembling tongues can find no words to say,
And eyes, bedazzled, dare not meet her gaze.

Modestly she goes amid the praise,
Serene and sweet, with virtue her array;

And seems a wonder sent here to display
A glimpse of heaven in an earthly place.

But, as Contini has explained,[9] all the terms I put in bold in the original had, in Dante's time, a different meaning, and a more philosophical one. *Gentile* did not mean, as in modern Italian, *courteous*, and in a way was closer to *gentle*, but in the sense of coming from a noble family. *Onesto* did not correspond to *honest* and meant rather *full of decorum and dignity* (in this sense Musa was 'honest'). *Donna* did not mean *woman* but *domina*, in the feudal sense, and in this context Beatrice was the *domina* of Dante's heart (*My lady* suggests something similar). *Pare* did not mean *she looks like* or *it seems that* but rather that the virtues of the Lady are *manifested evidently*, or that Beatrice is the visible manifestation of a miracle. Being a *cosa* Beatrice was not a *thing* but a *being* that produced sensations and emotions (in this sense two English translations employ *creature*, which is less philosophical but works pretty well, and Shores anticipates the final effect of that *cosa* saying that it is a *wonder*).

To conclude, according to Contini these lines should be paraphrased as 'Such is the evidence of the noble status and dignity of the person who is my Lady [...] She is going on, listening to words of praise, showing her own benevolence, and her nature of a being come from heaven to represent directly the divine power becomes evident.'

This is an instance in which readers of a modern translation can in some way understand the old sense of the poem a little better than modern Italian readers who believe their language has not changed since Dante's time. To take Dante as a contemporary could be to do seriously what Tony Oldcorn[10] tried as an intentional provocation:

When she says he, my baby looks so neat,
the fellas all clam up and check their feet.
She hears their whistles but she's such a cutie,
she walks on by, and no, she isn't snooty.
You'd think that she'd been sent down from the skies
to lay a little magic on us guys.

Translating Averroes

One of the most blatant examples of cultural misunderstanding, which has produced for at least some centuries a chain of further misconceptions, is that of Averroes' translation of Aristotle's *Poetics*. Averroes did not know Greek and hardly knew Syriac, and therefore read Aristotle through a tenth-century Arabic translation of a Syriac translation of the Greek original. To increase this mish-mash, Averroes' commentary to the *Poetics* (1175) was translated from Arabic into Latin by Hermann the German in 1256. Only later, in 1278, did William of Moerbeke translate the *Poetics* from Greek. As for Aristotle's *Rhetoric*, in 1256 Hermann the German translated it from an Arabic translation, mixing up the Aristotelian text with Arabic commentaries. Only later was there a *translatio vetus* directly from Greek, probably due to Bartholomew of Messina, and in 1269 or 1270 came the one by William of Moerbeke.

Aristotle's text is full of references to Greek theatre, as well as of poetical examples that Averroes and his forerunners had tried to adapt to the literary Arab tradition. Imagine how a Latin translator might picture the original sense of these two works. We are close to the situation of an English version of Genesis translated from a bad German translation translated in its turn from an incorrect Spanish version. But there is more than that.

Jorge Luis Borges, in his short story 'The Quest of Averroes' (*El Aleph*) shows Abulgualid Mohammed Ibn-Ahmed Ibn-Mohammed Ibn-Rushd (Averroes) as he tries to understand Aristotle's *Poetics*. He cannot catch the proper meaning of such words as *tragedy* and *comedy*, because such literary genres were alien to the Arab culture. The flavour of Borges's story is given by the fact that, while Averroes tortures his mind pondering the meaning of these obscure terms, in the courtyard below some children play: one of them imitates a muezzin, another pretends to be a minaret, and so on. They are performing a theatrical action, but neither they nor Averroes realise it. Later one of Averroes' guests recounts how he attended a strange ceremony in China, and from his description the readers (but certainly not the characters) realise that it was a drama. At the end,

Averroes again starts meditating on Aristotle and concludes: 'Aristù calls tragedy panegyrics and comedy satires and anathemas. The pages of the Koran as well as the inscriptions of the sanctuary are rich in tragedies and comedies.'

Readers are tempted to attribute such an ironic situation to the imagination of Borges, but what Borges narrates is exactly what really happened to Averroes. Everything Aristotle refers to as tragedy is referred to by Averroes as poetry, and mainly as the poetic genres of *vituperatio* and *laudatio*. Averroes says that this kind of epidictic poetry uses representations, but he means verbal representations, that can inspire virtuous actions. Obviously this moralising idea of poetry does not allow Averroes to understand the Aristotelian concept that the tragic action has a cathartic (rather than didactic) function.

At one point Averroes interprets the part of the *Poetics* where Aristotle lists the components of a tragedy: *mûthos, êthê, léxis, diánoia, ópsis* and *melopoiía* (usually translated as plot, characters, diction, reasoning, spectacle and song). Averroes translates the first four terms as 'mythical statement', 'character', 'metre' and 'beliefs' and the sixth as 'melody' (but he was certainly thinking of a poetic melody, not of the presence of musicians in the theatre). The real drama comes with the fifth component, *ópsis*. Averroes cannot think of staged actions and defines *ópsis* (or whatever his sources translated into Arabic) as an argument which demonstrates the moral validity of the represented beliefs. Hermann the German translates *argumentatio seu probatio rectitudinis credulitatis aut operationis*, and – misunderstanding the misunderstanding of Averroes – explains that such a *carmen laudativum* or eulogy does not use the art of gesticulation – so excluding the only really theatrical aspect of a tragedy.

When translating from Greek William of Moerbeke properly speaks of *tragodia* and *komodia* and seems aware of their theatrical nature. It is true that for medieval authors a comedy was a story with a happy end, so that even Dante's poem could be defined as a comedy; likewise, in his *Poetria Nova* John of Garland defined tragedy as a *carmen quod incipit a guadio et terminat in luctu*. In any case medieval culture knew the plays of jesters or *histriones*, and the holy mysteries, and so had an idea of theatre. Thus with Moerbeke, *ópsis* rightly becomes *visus*, and it is clear that that vision concerns the mimic action of the *ypocrita*, or actor. Moerbeke gives us a correct lexical interpretation because he knew an artistic genre that, in spite of many differences, medieval culture shared with the Greeks.

Some cases

I have always been intrigued by the possible Italian translations of the first verses of Valéry's 'Le cimetière marin':

> *Ce toit tranquille, où marchent des colombes,*
> *Entre les pins palpite, entre les tombes;*
> *Midi le juste y compose des feux*
> *La mer, la mer, toujours recommencée!*

It is evident that the *peaceful roof* where some or many *doves* walk is the sea, scattered with white sails, and if by chance the readers do not catch the metaphor of the first line, the fourth one offers them the key to a correct interpretation. That roof is *la mer*. However, in the process of disambiguation of a metaphor the reader usually starts from the verbal vehicle, but also puts many evoked images into play, and the first image that comes to mind when one thinks of the sea is that of a blue surface. Why should a roof be blue? Please note that such an image should disturb Latin readers most of all, since in Latin countries the roofs are red (including in Provence where the cemetery is situated). My answer to this conundrum is that Valéry, even though speaking of Provence (where he was born), was thinking as a Parisian. In Paris the roofs are made of slate, and under the sunlight give metallic reflections. When *midi le juste* arranges its fires on the marine surface it creates silvery glares which suggest to Valéry an expanse of Parisian roofs. I do not see any other reason for that metaphor and I realise that no translation can make it more perspicuous – not without a long paraphrase which would kill the rhythm and every other poetic effect.

Translators usually adopt for famous foreign cities the name used in their own country: thus London in Italian becomes *Londra* and Roma in English becomes *Rome*. There is no embarrassment in reading (in Italian) that Sherlock Holmes lives *in Londra*. But what does one do if in a Russian novel of Soviet times Kaliningrad is mentioned? Should it be translated in German as Königsberg? It becomes, I think, a matter of negotiation: if the Soviet novel tells a story that takes place in the time of Immanuel Kant, then Kaliningrad ought to be named Königsberg even in an English or Spanish translation. If on the contrary the novel represents events, feelings and ideas that refer to Soviet society, then Kaliningrad must remain Kaliningrad.

Source vs target

A translation can be either *source-* or *target-oriented*. These are the terms usually employed in translation studies. In other words, given a translation from Homer, should the translation transform its readers into Greek readers of Homeric times or should it make Homer write as if he were writing today in our language? The question is not as preposterous as it seems, when we consider that translations age. Dante's *Divine Comedy*, in Italian, is always the same, but if modern French readers read a Dantesque translation from the nineteenth century they feel uncomfortable. Translators, even when trying to give us the flavour of a language and of a historical period, are in fact *modernising* their source.

I want to refrain from considering questions that, according to me, have more to do with comparative literature than with translation theory, namely, to what extent certain translations have obliged a given language to express thoughts and facts that it was not accustomed to express before. The translations from Heidegger have, over recent decades, radically changed the French philosophical style; in Italy, before the Second World War, the first translations of American writers made by Elio Vittorini (frequently very unfaithful both from a lexical and grammatical point of view, since he misunderstood many American idioms) contributed to the creation of a new Italian narrative style that triumphed after the war as a new form of realism. It is extremely important to study the role of translation within the context of a receiving culture, but from this point of view a translation becomes a purely internal affair between the target language and all the linguistic and cultural problems posed by the original. In this sense one should take a stylistically awkward translation full of lexical mistakes, but which has greatly influenced generations of readers and writers, more seriously than one that critics would define as more correct.

Luther[11] used the verbs *übersetzen* (to translate) and *verdeutschen* (to Germanise) as synonymous (thus making evident the importance of a translation as *cultural assimilation*), and answered some of the critics of his German translation of the Bible by saying 'They are learning to speak and write German from my translation, and so in a sense stealing my language, which they hardly knew a word of before.'

But this has nothing to do with the study of the process from a source text to a target text, which ought to be considered from a different point of view: should a translation lead the reader to understand the linguistic and cultural universe of the source text, or transform the original by adapting it to the reader's cultural and linguistic universe?

Foreignising and domesticating

The difference between *modernising* the text and *keeping it archaic* is not the same as the one between *foreignising* and *domesticating* it. Even though there are many translations in which both oppositions are in play, let me consider first of all the opposition of foreignising vs domesticating.[12]

Probably the most blatant example of a reader-oriented or domesticating translation is Luther's. For example, discussing the best way to translate *Ex abundantia cordis os loquitur* from Matthew 12:34, he remarks:

If I followed those jackasses, they would probably set the letters before me and have me translate it 'out of the abundance of the heart the mouth speaketh'. Tell me, is that how any real person would speak? . . . What on earth is 'the abundance of the heart'? . . . What the mother in her house and the common man would say is something like: 'speak straight from the heart!'

Apropos the expressions *Ut quid perditio haec?* (Matthew 26:8) and *Ut quid perditio ista unguenti facta est?* (Mark 14:4) he says:

If I followed those lemmings the literalists, I'd have to render that latter question 'Why was this waste of the ointment made?' What kind of talk is that? Whoever talks about 'making a waste of the ointment'? You make a mess, not a waste, and anybody who heard you talking about making a waste would naturally think you were actually making something, when in fact you are unmaking it – though that still sounds pretty vague (nobody unmakes a waste either) . . . What a real person would say, of course, is 'What a waste!', or 'What a shame to waste that ointment!' Then the listener would understand that Mary Magdalene has squandered the ointment, at least according to Judas, who would have been more sparing with it.[13]

Humboldt[14] proposed a difference between *Fremdheit* (which can be translated as *foreignness, unfamiliarity, strangeness, alienness*) and *das Fremde* (usually translated as *the strange* or *the unfamiliar*). Maybe the two terms were not so well chosen, but the concept is clear: readers feel *Fremdheit* when the translator's choice sounds strange, as if it were a mistake; they feel *das Fremde*, that is, an unfamiliar way of showing something that is recognisable, when they get the impression they are seeing it for the first time, under a different guise. I think that this concept is not so different from the notion of *ostrannenija* or 'defamiliarisation' proposed by Russian Formalists: a device by which an artist succeeds in persuading his readers to perceive the described object under a different light and to understand it better than before. The example provided by Humboldt supports my reading:

A translation cannot and should not be a commentary ... The obscurity one sometimes finds in the writings of the ancients, most especially the *Agamemnon*, is born of the brevity and the boldness with which, scorning connective clauses, they string together thoughts, images, feelings, memories and intuitions as they arise out of a profoundly agitated soul. The more thoroughly one penetrates the mood of a poet, his period, his characters, the more the obscurity vanishes and is replaced by a high clarity.

These problems are crucial in the translation of remote texts. As far as modern literature is concerned, the options can vary. Should an English translation from a French novel speak of the Left Bank or *la rive gauche*? Short[15] finds a funny example in the tender French appellation *mon petit chou*. If one translates literally as *my little cabbage* the expression could sound insulting. Short suggests *sweetheart* but admits that this misses the humorous contrast, the affectionate nuance and the sound of *chou* ('or even the way the lips must be shaped to make that sound'). Certainly *sweetheart* is a good example of domesticating translation, but if the scene takes place in France I think that one should preserve the French expression. Perhaps the reader will not understand the right meaning of those sounds but they will probably detect something very French-like, and would guess that this is how French people speak when they are in love.

Sometimes domestication is unavoidable. Bill Weaver has written a 'Pendulum Diary', reporting day by day the problems he met in translating my *Foucault's Pendulum*.[16] One of his recurrent problems concerned tenses.

When the narrator intervenes, Umberto uses regularly – or rather, irregularly – the pluperfect ('he had gone') when in English, it seems to me, the past ('he went') is more likely. As always in translating Italian narrative, and especially Eco's, the various layers of the past have to be rethought. Just as some of the future verbs have to be altered, usually to conditional.

Thus Weaver was obliged to reconsider the various temporal levels of my stories, especially when, in the *Pendulum*, he was facing a character who remembers different temporal phases in a continuous interplay of embedded flashbacks.

There are cases in which Weaver, to make something evident to his target reader had to change the text – as happened with Dotallevi's hedge (mentioned in my chapter 3). Weaver cites chapter 107 of the *Pendulum* where, during a nightmarish car trip through the mountains with his lover Lorenza, Belbo – passing through a lost village – runs over a dog. Nobody knows to whom the poor animal belongs and Belbo and Lorenza are obliged to waste the whole afternoon trying to assist the unfortunate beast, without really knowing what to do.

At a certain point, Belbo and Lorenzo having looked impotently at the moaning creature for more than an hour, my text says: *Uggiola, aveva detto Belbo, cruscante* ... *Uggiola* means *whimpers* but it is certainly not such a common word in ordinary Italian. That's why I added *cruscante* – which means that Belbo followed the classical prescriptions of the Crusca Dictionary, which for centuries represented and still represents a model for the Italian language.

Bill Weaver realised this point and in fact he comments.

Belbo says *Uggiola*, using an arcane, literary word. But in English 'whimper' is not arcane at all. So to maintain the *à toujours litteraire* character of Belbo, I make him quote Eliot. "'He's whimpering,'" Belbo said, and then, with Eliot-like detachment: "He's ending with a whimper."'

I approved Bill's choice. Now, on second thoughts, and after having just read Weaver's comments, I realise that my erudite allusion was very light (the reader could overlook it) while the English text makes the allusion much too evident. If I had to advise my translator now I would suggest to him to translate only: *He's ending with a whimper, Belbo said* ... – without any explicit reference to Eliot. If the reader catches the reference, it couldn't be better; if not, too bad. But I shall speak more on similar problems in one of my next essays, apropos intertextual irony.

Another interesting case concerns chapter 66 of *Foucault's Pendulum* where – to make fun of the occultists and their inclination to interpret any word, image, event or thing of this world as a hermetic allusion to a Secret – Belbo shows Casaubon that it is possible to identify mystic symbols even in the structure of a car. So he interprets the axle of a car as an allusion to the Sephirotic Tree of the Kabbalah.

For the English translator the game was not so easy, because in Italian we use the word *albero*, tree, both for the Kabbalistic symbol and for the axle of a car – while in English the verbal analogy disappears. Happily, consulting technical dictionaries, Weaver found out that even for cars it is technically possible to speak of an *axle-tree*. Thus he could translate this parodistic allusion in a way that created a similar effect. However, he encountered an embarrassing problem when he met the line:

Per questo i figli della Gnosi dicono che non bisogna fidarsi degli Ilici ma degli Pneumatici.

Here my play was perhaps too sophomoric and rather difficult to understand, even for an Italian. In the Gnostic tradition there is a distinction between Hylics and Pneumatics, that is, between material and spiritual people. By a happy coincidence in Italian *pneumatici* also means tyres (which is etymologically correct, since tyres are inflated with an aerial essence). In this way my joke was acceptable and allowed Belbo to demonstrate once more that a car can be seen as an encyclopaedia of occult wisdom. But in English the joke was absolutely untranslatable.

As Weaver says in his diary, while together having a sort of brainstorming about a possible solution, he mentioned a famous tyre brand, Firestone, and I reacted – by phonic association – with *philosopher's stone*. That was the solution, and the line became:

They never saw the connection between the philosopher's stone and Firestone.

The choice between foreignising or domesticating is really a matter of careful negotiation.

Sometimes Weaver's solutions were the result of curious discussions with my wife (who is German-born):

At one point in the novel Belbo says to Casaubon, in English: *Good for you.* In his instructions to translators Umberto gives strict orders against the solution of an asterisk and 'English in the original' . . . I suggested changing Belbo's line to *Bon pour vous.* After a moment's thought, Umberto said: 'Put *Wunderbar.*'

I was not convinced – and I tell this to Renate, who says: 'No, no. Put *bon pour vous.* No Italian publisher would have said *Wunderbar* in those days.'

In Gide's translation of Conrad's *Typhoon*, in the second chapter a character says *He didn't care a tinker's curse.* Gide translates *Il s'en fichait comme du juron d'un étameur.* This is more or less literally correct but does not recall any known French idiom. In the sixth chapter a character utters *Damme, if this ship isn't worse than Bedlam!* Gide, consistently with his foreignising project, translates *Que le diable m'emporte si l'on se croyait pas à Bedlam!*

Berman[17] quotes an objection that it would have been better to say *Il s'en fichait comme d'une guigne*, hence using a typical slang French expression, and to substitute Bedlam with Charenton (a French asylum), but he remarks that it would be strange if British characters were to use French idioms.

Certainly *Charenton* would be an excessive case of domestication, but I do not know if a French reader would have felt a reference to *guigne* too 'local' or 'national'. I cannot but praise two Italian translators (Ugo Mursia and Bruno Oddera)[18] who respectively chose for the first case *Non gli importava un cavolo* and *Non gli importava un fico secco* – two very slang expressions that say the same thing and that the reader does not feel are too Italian – and for the second case, *Maledizione, se questa nave non è peggio del manicomio di Bedlam* and *Il diavolo mi porti se questa nave non è peggio di un manicomio* – the first one specifying that Bedlam is a mental hospital and the second mentioning only an asylum in general, without any further reference.

An interesting case of domestication in order to foreignise is the one mentioned by my Croatian translator, Morana Čale Kneževic.[19] *The Name of the Rose* is rich (perhaps too rich) in intertextual references, but for many of the texts I evoked there was no Croatian version. Therefore Čale Kneževic translated the quotation as it appeared in Italian (counting, as she says, on the ability of her readers to discover echoes of their previous readings in foreign languages). For other texts she discovered that analogous quotations appeared in other works translated into Croatian and decided to quote the texts as they appeared in these translations and not necessarily as they were in Italian. She realised that in the Prologue I was evoking the *topos* of the *Monde renversé*, the world turned upside down, through quotations from a medieval text, *Carmina Burana*, but in prose, as they were cited in Curtius's seminal book on European literature and medieval Latin. As far as I was concerned I had the *Carmina Burana* before me, but I had certainly been inspired by Curtius too, so Morana's insight was good. But she remarked that the Croatian translation of Curtius contained a quotation which is different from both Curtius's German original and the Latin original, so also different from my quotation in *The Name of the Rose*. In spite of this she decided to keep the Croatian version, even though non-literal, in order to arouse in her readers' minds a sort of intertextual (and familiar) connection.

I feel obliged to approve this kind of choice. If the aim of the text was to draw the reader into recognising quotations from other texts, in order to 'smell' a sort of archaic flavour, a certain rate of domestication was indispensable. By the way, in my novel I do not say that Adso was literally quoting from *Carmina Burana*: it is verisimilar that, as a character in the Middle Ages, he was vaguely remembering certain texts and echoing them without any philological preoccupation. In a way the Croatian Adso was more medieval than the Italian one.

Among my translators, Kroeber is the one who has most bravely accepted the necessity of domestication – or, as a good disciple of Luther, of Germanisation.[20] He was aware of the syntactic differences between Italian and German and of the fact that many Italian expressions, still used today, can seem archaic to a German reader. When translating *The Name of the Rose* he decided that many of those sylistic features, typical of a medieval chronicle, had to be preserved. Kroeber was thinking of the style used by Thomas Mann in his 'Joseph' trilogy. But Adso was not just a medieval character, he was a German medieval character, and in German such a characteristic had to be evident. Kroeber asked himself how to reconstruct Adso's stylistic 'mask' in a German style. He confesses that when in my dialogues I used *dissi* or *disse* (that is, *I said* and *he said*), he resorted to the whole gamut of German *turn ancillaries* like *versetze ich, erwirdert er, gab er zu bedenken* – 'because so the traditional German narrator used to do'.

Kroeber admits that when playing such a game one is tempted to overdo things. Thus, in translating the episode of Adso's dream (see previous chapter) he not only respected all the references to the *Coena Cypriani* and to various aspects of medieval literature and art, but also referred to some of his personal literary memories: he even inserted vague allusions to Mann and Brecht – this was not unfaithful to my original text, because I inserted allusions to Wittgenstein. Kroeber seems to apologise, in speaking of these solutions, because his translation was 'belle' but 'infidèle'. I think that, if his purpose was to create in the mind of German readers the same effect that I tried to create in the mind of the Italian one, he was not unfaithful at all.

Modernising and making a text archaic

As for the opposition between modernising the text and making it archaic, let us consider various translations of the book of the Bible known as Ecclesiastes. I shall consider the canonical Latin translation, the King James and Luther versions, and some contemporary versions, in French and in Italian (one by Chouraqui, one by Erri de Luca and two different versions by Ceronetti).[21]

The original Hebrew title is *Qohèlèt*, which could be a proper name but also recalls the Hebrew etym *qahal*, assembly. Thus *Qohèlèt* can even be one who speaks in the assembly of the faithful. The Greek term for assembly is *ekklesia*, and Ecclesiastes was the title chosen by the Vulgata and still accepted by the King James version. But in King James *Qohèlèt* is translated as *The Preacher*, and similarly in Luther's translation it becomes *der Predigter*. The English and German translations are clearly modernising.

Let us come to the famous second verse:

Vanitas vanitatum, dixit Ecclesiastes. Vanitas vanitatum et omnia vanitas. (Vulgata)

Vanity of vanities, saith the Preacher, vanity of vanities; all is vanity. (King James)

Es is ganz eitel, sprach der Predigter, es ist alles ganz eitel. (Luther)

Fumée de fumée, dit Qohèlèt: fumée de fumée, tout est fumée. (Chouraqui)

Spreco di sprechi ha detto Kohèlet, spreco di sprechi il tutto è spreco. (De Luca)

Fumo di fumi – Dice Qohélet – Fumo di fumi – Tutto non è che fumo. (Ceronetti 2001)

The invective against *vanitas* is obviously against what is inconsistent and null, and the words *vanitas, vanity, vanità, Eitel* suggested the right concept, at least at the time in which the translations were made. Today the original sense has been lost, and readers think of vanity as excessive care for one's own public image. Thus, working on the original Hebrew metaphor, Chouraqui and Ceronetti speak of *fumée*, smoke, and De Luca of *spreco*, waste. Their solution is poetically convincing but they miss the old sense of vanity as void and unreality.

As for the verse *Oritur sol, et occidit, et ad locum suum revertitur: ibique renascens* (Vulgata), the translations are:

The sun also ariseth, and the sun goeth down, and hasteth to his place where he arose. (King James)

Die Sonne geth auf und geth unter und läuft an ihren Ort, dass sie wieder dasselbst aufgehe. (Luther)

Le soleil brille, le soleil décline: à son lieu il aspire et brille là. (Chouraqui)

E è spuntato il sole e se n'è venuto il sole: e al suo luogo ansima, spunta lui là. (De Luca)
Corre in un altro punto – In un altro riappare. (Ceronetti 1970)

The solutions of both Chouraqui and De Luca are syntactically tortured (these verses are neither in good French nor in good Italian), in order to convey or suggest the flavour of an exotic poetical style. Both Chouraqui and De Luca are at once foreignising the text and making it archaic.

Mixed situations

The double opposition, foreignising/domesticating and modernising/making it archaic, can produce a range of possible combinations. In my *The Name of the Rose* there are frequent quotations and book titles in Latin. I had in mind Western readers who were in some way acquainted with Latin expressions even if they had not studied Latin.

But my Russian translator, Helena Costiukovich, remarked that Latin words (whether or not transliterated in Cyrillic characters) are not only incomprehensible to Russian readers, but also do not convey any religious connotation. Thus Costiukovich decided to render my Latin quotations in the old ecclesiastic Slavonic used by the orthodox Church in the Middle Ages – so that the reader could both vaguely understand their meaning and perceive the same aura of old religiosity. Thus, in order to make the translation very archaic, it was necessary to domesticate it.

Likewise, Venuti[22] quotes the debate between Matthew Arnold and Francis Newman (in the nineteenth century) apropos translating Homer. Arnold said that Homer should be rendered in hexameters and in modern English, in order to keep the translation in tune with the current academic reception of the Greek text; Newman, by contrast, not only constructed an archaic lexicon but also used an old ballad meter, in order to show that Homer was originally a popular rather than elitist poet. Venuti remarks that, ironically, Newman was foreignising for populist reasons and Arnold wanted to domesticate for academic and elitist reasons.

A crazy example of both domestication and modernisation is given by the first tentative translation of one of my essays. Happily that translation was corrected before publication.

My text discussed the *Ars Magna* of Raymond Lull, and the subject was certainly a difficult one. My text was listing a series of Lullian syllogisms on theological matters, among which was *All that is magnified by Greatness is great – but Goodness is what is magnified by Greatness – therefore Goodness is Great.*

The translator probably thought that the Lullian reasoning was too abstract and that it was necessary to be more friendly to the reader. Thus he translated the above syllogism as *All cats are mammals, Suzy is a cat, therefore Suzy is a mammal.* It is clear that this translation is not literal at all. Moreover, it does not respect what the original was referring to. To say that a historical figure like Lull said that *All that is magnified by Greatness is great* is pretty different from saying that he mentioned his pet Suzy. A translator can say that Diotallevi (a ficitonal character) saw a *sublime espacioso llano* instead of a hedge, but not that Raymond Lull spoke of Suzy instead of God. That is a blatant lie, and the reader becomes the victim of a fraud. Besides Lull was a Catalan and would have never named his cat Suzy.

One could conclude that my translator simply exaggerated in modernisation and domestication. But his misdemeanour was born from an insufficient appreciation of the deep sense of my text: I was doing my best to initiate the modern reader into the cultural world of Lull, and such a show of goodwill should not be undervalued.

Schleiermacher once said:

> The translator either disturbs the writer as little as possible and moves the reader in his direction, or disturbs the reader as little as possible and moves the writer in his direction. The two approaches are so absolutely different that no mixture of the two is to be trusted.[23]

I repeat that such a severe criterion perhaps holds for translation from ancient or remote literatures, but that it does not hold for modern texts. To choose a target- or source-oriented direction is, once again, a matter of negotiation to be decided at every sentence.

In American crime novels the detective frequently asks a driver to take him downtown or uptown. By a sort of unspoken agreement, all Italian translators have decided to translate these expressions as *portami alla Città Alta*, that is, to the high or upper city, or *portami alla Città Bassa*, that is, to the low or lower city. Thus Italian readers get the impression that every American city is like Budapest or Tbilisi, with a district on the hills beyond the river, and a district on the opposite bank.

It is certainly difficult to decide how to translate *downtown* and *uptown*, because the sense of these expressions changes according to the city concerned. Normally uptown is north and downtown is south, but in certain cities downtown is the oldest district, in others it is the business area, in others the red-light district. In New York, downtown and uptown are relative concepts: if you are escaping a black gang in Harlem you ask the driver to run downtown in order to reach at least the Plaza; if you are on the verge of being killed in Chinatown, you ask the driver to run as fast as possible uptown, so as to relax at the Plaza. The Plaza is neither uptown nor downtown: which it is depends not on the Plaza's position but on yours.

A good translator should therefore negotiate the translation according to the city, asking the driver to take him to the business district, or to the red-light one, or along the river or elsewhere, according to the situation. But these decisions require vast extra-linguistic knowledge, and translators of detective novels are poorly paid. My suggestion is that one should foreignise and use *downtown*, in English, to give the tale an exotic connotation (and the reader will understand later whether it was wise or not to go there). If you read a criminal story taking place in Barcelona (where you have never been) and you read *Take me to the Barrio Gotico*, do you really understand what it means? Certainly, there is a great difference between going (especially at night) to the Barrio Gotico or to the Barrio Chino, but too bad. Better to get the exotic flavour of Barcelona than to receive ill-translated information. So, if an English translator finds *Take me to the Barrio Chino* in a Spanish novel, it is advisable not to translate this as *Take me to Chinatown*. Exaggerated domestication can bring excessive obscurity.

Besides, translators in every language have their own downtown problems. In his 'Pendulum Diary' Bill Weaver reports a similar story.

> Thought for the day. *Periferia*. Outskirts. In most Italian cities, the *periferia* is the slums. In American cities, nowadays, the slums are downtown, the 'inner city'. So when you say someone lives *in periferia*, you have to watch yourself and not translate it as 'in the suburbs', making an Italian slum sound like Larchmont. Casaubon lives and works in an ex-factory *in periferia*. I've eluded the problem, I think, by using 'outlying'.

As a matter of fact in Italy one can live at the *periferia* of a small non-industrial city and have a comfortable little house with a garden. But Casaubon lived in Milan and Weaver did well in avoiding *suburbs*. Casaubon was not rich enough.

In conclusion, Montanari[24] suggests translating *source/target* as *source/mouth*. Perhaps *mouth* is better than *target*, which sounds too businesslike, and conveys an impossible idea of optimal scoring. But the idea of *mouth* also opens a semantic field and suggests the form either of a delta or an estuary. Perhaps there are source texts that widen out in translation, and the destination text enriches the source one, making it enter the sea of a new intertextuality; and there are delta texts that branch out in many translations, each of which impoverishes their original flow, but which all together create a new territory, a labyrinth of competing interpretations.

NOTES

1. Willard Van Orman Quine, *Word and Object* (Cambridge: M.I.T. Press, 1960).
2. José Ortega y Gasset, *Miseria y esplendor de la traducción*, (*Obras completa*, V), (Madrid: Revista de Occidente, 1947), pp. 427–48. English. tr., 'The misery and the splendor of translation', in Lawrence Venuti, ed., *The Translation Studies Reader* (London: Routledge, 2000), pp. 56–77.
3. 'Uber die verschiedenen Methoden des Übersetzens,' (1813), in *Zur Philosophie* 2 (Berlin: Reimer, 1835–46). English tr., 'On the different methods of translating', in Douglas Robinson, ed., *Western Translation Theory* (Manchester: St Jerome Publishing, 1997), pp. 226–7.
4. 'Einleitung', in *Aeschylos Agamemnon metrisch Übersetz* (Leipzig: Fleischer, 1816). English tr., 'The more faithful, the more divergent', in Robinson, ed., pp. 238–40.
5. George Steiner, *After Babel* (London: Oxford U.P. 1975).
6. *Dante and His Circle with the Italian Poets Preceding Him* (London: Ellis, 1908) (originally as *The Early Italian Poets*, 1861).
7. *Dante's 'Vita Nuova'* (Bloomington: Indiana U.P., 1973).
8. *The Formalist*, 1 (1992), p. 73.
9. Gianfranco Contini, 'Esercizio d'interpretazione sopra un sonetto di Dante', *Varianti e altra linguistica* (Torino: Einaudi, 1979), pp. 61–8.
10. 'Confessioni di un falsario', in Franco Nasi, ed., *Sulla traduzione letteraria* (Ravenna: Longo, 2001), p. 68.
11. Martin Luther, *Sendbrief von Dolmetschen* 1530. English tr., 'Circular

letter on translation', in Robinson, ed., pp. 83–8.

12. See Lawrence Venuti, *The Translator's Invisibility* (London: Routledge, 1995).

13. 'Circular letter on translation', p. 87.

14. 'Einleitung', p. 240.

15. Thomas L. Short, 'Peirce on meaning and translation', in Susan Petrilli, ed., *La traduzione*, special issue of *Athanor* x, 2 (1999–2000), p. 78.

16. 'Pendulum Diary', in *South-West Review*, Spring 1990.

17. Antoine Berman, *La traduction et la lettre ou l'auberge lointain*, second edn. (Paris: Seuil, 1999), p. 65, quoting Van der Meercschen, 'La traduction française, problèmes de fidelité', in *Traduzione Tradizione* (Milano: Dedalo, 1986), p. 80.

18. '*Typhoon* di Joseph Conrad nella traduzione di André Gide con versione italiana di Ugo Mursia', (Torino: Einaudi, 1993); *Tifone*, tr. Bruno Oddera (Milano: Bompiani, 1986).

19. Morana Čale Knežević, 'Traduzione, tradizione e tradimento: in margine alla versione croata de *Il nome della rosa*', in Avirovič and Dodds, eds., *Umberto Eco, Claudio Magris. Autori e traduttori a confronto* (*Trieste, 27–8 novembre 1989*) (Udine: Campanotto, 1993), pp. 47–53.

20. Burckhart Kroeber, 'Stare al gioco dell'autore', in Avirovič and Dodds, pp. 27–30.

21. *La Bible*, tr. André Chouraqui (Desclée de Brouwer, 1989). *Kohèlet. Ecclesiaste*, tr. Erri De Luca (Milano: Feltrinelli, 1996). *Qohélet o l'Ecclesiaste*, tr. Guido Ceronetti (Torino: Einaudi, 1970). *Qohélet. Colui che prende la parola*, tr. Guido Ceronetti (Milano: Adelphi, 2001).

22. Lawrence Venuti, 'Strategies of translation', in Mona Baker, ed., *Routledge Encyclopedia of Translation Studies* (London: Routledge, 1998), p. 240.

23. 'On the different methods of translating', p. 229.

24. Frederico Montanari, 'Tradurre metafore?', in N. Dusi and S. Nergaard, eds., *Sulla traduzione intersemiotica*, special issue of *VS* lxxxv–lxxxvii (2000).

FIVE

To see things and texts

In writing my novels I have always been interested in the description of spaces, so that usually, before writing, I carefully design the world where my story will take place. I want my characters to move within a space that, in some way, I can see. But in order to write about spaces it is not enough to see a space: the real problem is how to render what one sees in words. This is the problem of *hypotyposis*.

Hypotyposis

Hypotyposis is the rhetorical effect by which words succeed in rendering a visual scene. Unfortunately all the rhetoricians who wrote about hypotyposis, from antiquity to the present, have provided only circular definitions. They have said more or less that hypotyposis is the figure by which one creates a visual effect through words – that is, in order to answer the question, they have restated the question as if it was the answer. Requested to say *how* it happens, they have simply repeated *that* it happens.

In the past few years I have analysed many literary texts in order to isolate different techniques by which a writer, using sounds, brings images, so to speak, to the reader's eyes, and I particularly focused my attention on the description of spaces.

Most of these techniques do not require any effort on the part of the translator. The simplest, most immediate and mechanical form is pure *mentioning*, as when we say that two places are twenty miles distant from each other. The second is detailed description, that is, when a space is *described*, as when we talk about a square with a church on the right and an ancient building on the left.

The third form is *listing*. In a list or catalogue space is shown by the accumulation of things it contains. Good examples of catalogues can be found in classical literature: see for instance the description of the armies before Troy in the *Iliad*, which is a catalogue of names that lasts four hundred verses, or the description of the drawers in Leopold Bloom's kitchen in the penultimate chapter of *Ulysses*.

Another technique (which Quintilian suggested in his *Institutio Oratoria*) is the agitated *piling up* of events. The events must be either incongruous or extraordinary. Of course rhythm is very important here, and that is how this hypotyposis from Rabelais (*Gargantua* I, 27) makes us see the scene, which would not be possible with a mere listing device:

> He crushed to a pulp the head of some, broke the arms and legs of other ones, dislocated the neck vertebrae of a third one, or he broke the loins, cut the nose, split the eyes, smashed the lower jaws, made them swallow their teeth, battered the omoplates, smashed the legs, separated the limbs from the body [and so on for more than one page, finishing with] ... Some died without speaking, others spoke without dying; some died while speaking, others spoke while dying...

In such cases we must ask the translator to pay attention to the verbal rhythm, which is crucial in this kind of stylistic device.

An interesting technique is that which I decided to define as *fractalisation of space at an ant's pace*. This idea was suggested to me by Eliot, when in 'The Love Song of J. Alfred Prufrock' he writes:

> The yellow fog that rubs its back upon the window-panes,
> The yellow smoke that rubs its muzzle on the window-panes,
> Licked its tongue into the corners of the evening,
> Lingered upon the pools that stand in drains,
> Let fall upon its back the soot that falls from chimneys,
> Slipped by the terrace, made a sudden leap,
> And seeing that it was a soft October night,
> Curled once about the house, and fell asleep.

In this case, whereas the human traveller would walk on too quickly to see what the London walls and street corners really look like, the reader is asked to imagine the speed at which fog moves. This involves slowing down the reading pace and passing by all wall recesses and window edges – just as would happen if we were asked to imagine how an ant walks through the *tourniquets* of a tiny space which we can cover, in an instant, with our feet.

In pondering about hypotyposis I felt the compulsion to write a novel in which the main characters were space and light. So I started to write *The Island of the Day Before.* My first idea was to put a shipwreck victim on a boat, in sight of an island that he was unable to reach. I wanted to tell a story of spaces (and light), and in order to keep my space untouched I want to write a story of an insuperable distance. That is why I decided that my main character had to be unable to swim.

To represent a character who cannot swim from here to there in a few strokes, but can only move through innumerable and unbearable efforts, was a way of demonstrating that fractalisation of space that I admired so much in Eliot. Thus my character, trying to swim, and only gaining a few feet at each attempt, always remained far from the island that, instead of approaching, shrank back at every effort. If in the course of this process one keeps describing the sea and the image of the coast, then one provides one's readers with the experience of a continuously broadening space.

Even this technique does not give a translator great problems. The only difficulty is in describing many different things in the course of the continuous effort of the swimmer, and I examined that problem in one of my previous essays, apropos the variety of colours and coral that the translators were asked to render.

But what interests me today is a very peculiar technique, by means of which a visual situation is evoked through an appeal to the reader's personal experiences. This technique asks the addressee to cooperate with the text by evoking some of his/her past experiences. It triggers not only pre-existing cognitive patterns but also pre-existing body experiences.

The difficulties for the translator are due to the fact that while a text can evoke a personal experience with a single word, this word does not have the same evocative impact every time, in every culture or country. I remember that once, in order to describe a poor and abandoned place in an underdeveloped country, I told my friends that it looked like Hiroshima in August 1945. My interlocutors understood what I meant perfectly because each of them vividly remembered many images of that event. I wonder if young people – not in a century, probably even today – can give a visual interpretation to my quotation.

There are two verses from the *Prose du transsiberien* by Blaise Cendrars that I like very much (it is a poem which, dealing with a very long journey, makes use of many different techniques for representing an unending space experienced over an unending time). At one point Cendrars recalls that:

Toutes les femmes que j'ai rencontrées se dressent aux horizons
Avec les gestes piteux et les regards tristes des sémaphores sous la
    pluie . . .

Those who are still familiar with old slow train journeys on foggy nights will be able to evoke these phantasmagorical shapes which slowly disappear and almost dissolve in the drizzle, in the gasping rhythm of the train. But I am afraid that a young reader accustomed to contemporary express trains with hermetically sealed windows cannot have had the experience of leaning out of the window to follow in the dark the vanishing of some ghostly signal. (Even the trilingual warning against leaning out has now disappeared from the cars.) How can one respond to a hypotyposis stirring the memory of something one has never seen? I think however that a text can frequently encourage its readers to *imagine* having seen something. The two verses by Cendrars appear in a context in which a train is described that travels for many days across vast terrains; the 'gestures' of these unknown semaphores are named, the horizons are mentioned, readers are asked to evoke situations in which imprecise forms loom in the dark or in the fog; even from a fast express train today one can still perceive some glimmer disappearing in the night ... A good hypotyposis can also create the memory that it needs in order to occur.

The really puzzling problem arises in the Italian translation of these verses. One must translate the French *semaphores* as *semafori* in Italian – there is no other way to do it. Now in French a semaphore is, more or less as in English, an apparatus for signalling, sometimes by one or more movable arms, and in French it normally refers to systems of communication in the navy and more specifically along a railway. Thus one would not confuse semaphores with traffic lights. Now, in Italian *semaforo* has the double meaning of semaphore and traffic light, but it is more commonly used for traffic lights. Traffic lights are in a city and are luminous signals, while the *gestes piteux* mentioned by Cendrars seem to evoke the movement of the mechanical arms of the railway system. Moreover, the very notion of horizon changes if one thinks of city streets instead of an unlimited countryside landscape. I do not see any way to escape this difficulty and I would assume that in general Cendrars' verses provoke in Italian a different visual effect from in French or in English. I must confess that, as a reader, for a long time I saw in these verses a flickering, a blinking of red eyes, more than the pitiful gestures of a desperate marionette.

In the course of my translation of *Sylvie* I found cases in which Nerval uses terms that must have been familiar to readers of his day, but may be obscure for modern readers, even modern French readers. In chapter 6, where Sylvie and the Narrator visit Sylvie's old aunt at Othys, there is a kind of enchanted return to the preceding century: the aunt allows her niece to go into her bedroom and rummage among the mementos of her youth, at the time of her marriage to Sylvie's uncle (by that time dead), and we have as it were an epiphany of late eighteenth-century pastoral-genteel kitsch. But in order to realise what Sylvie and her friend discover we need to understand some archaic terms, connected with the fashions of those far-off days, which Nerval's contemporaries certainly still understood.

At this point the translator ought to behave as if he or she were a director who means to transpose the story into film. But the translator cannot use either images or detailed specifications, and must respect the rhythm of the story.

In an old portrait discovered in the room, Sylvie's old aunt appears as a young girl *élancée dans son corsage ouvert à échelle de rubans*. Here are three English translations:

Halévy: . . . attractive and lissom in her open corsage crossed with ribbons . . .

Aldington: . . . slender in her open corset with its crossed ribbons . . .

Sieburth: . . . slender in her open bodice laced with ribbons . . .

The various Italian translators proposed *corpetto aperto sul davanti a nastri incrociati; corpetto dai nastri a zig-zag; corpetto, aperto coi nastri incrociati sul davanti; camicetta aperta a scala di nastri; corpetto aperto a scala di nastri; corsetto aperto sotto la scala dei nastri; corsetto aperto a nastri scalati; corpetto aperto in volantini di nastri; corsetto aperto a scala di nastri; corpetto aperto ed allacciato dai nastri incrociati sul davanti.* One can see that Italian translators tried bravely, but without success, to render *échelle de rubans*, while English translators gave up on ladders and staircases and mentioned only laced or crossed ribbons. But how open was that bodice or corset? Such a detail is rather relevant since the topic of that scene is the subtle and malicious charm of the aunt at the time of her glorious youth.

Now, a *corsage à echelle de rubans* is a bodice with a generous scoop neck that goes at least as far as the first swelling of the bosom and is fastened by a series of bows of decreasing size to form a wasp waist. An example is to be seen in Boucher's portrait of Madame de Pompadour.

This corset is certainly coquettish and elegant: it gives a generous view of the bosom and tapers down to form a seductively narrow waist – and this is what counts. For this reason I preferred to translate as *slanciata nel suo corsetto dalla vasta scollatura serrato a vespa da grandi nastri* (that is, a corset with a deep scoop neck fastened by large ribbons to form a wasp waist) – and that the ribbons are in scale ought to be suggested by the fact that the corset fastening gets progressively narrower towards the waist.

The French expression contained nine words. The three English translations have respectively ten, nine and eight words. Mine has thirteen. That is certainly too many from the rhythmic point of view, but I felt that this aural loss was necessary in order to gain visual precision. This was for me an interesting case of negotiation. The relevant element in that visualisation was the exciting and seductive waistline of the young bride, and it was that that I had to make visible, thus abandoning any effort to translate literally. At the same time my solution represented an effort to make the translation archaic, that is, to put the modern reader in the situation of a contemporary of Nerval.

Ekphrasis

I shall deal in my next essays with many cases of so-called intersemiotic translation, that is, of transposition from a given semiotic system to another, as happens when a novel is transformed into a movie or a painting is described by a poem. When a verbal text describes a work of visual art, classic tradition spoke of ekphrasis, a specific literary genre, which has a venerable pedigree. Note that many visual works of the past are known today only through the verbal descriptions given by ekphrasis.

Today ekphrasis is no longer celebrated as a literary *tour de force*, but many pages of art criticism are good examples of ekphrasis, as is the description of Velazquez's *Meninas* at the beginning of *Les mots et les choses* by Foucault.

As a matter of fact, even today, many poems and stories begin life as the description of a visual work. But authors usually conceal their source, or are at least not preoccupied with making it explicit. I shall characterise these cases as examples of *occult* ekphrasis.

Classical (and explicit) ekphrasis was meant to be appreciated as a good description of a painting or of a statue. Modern occult ekphrasis aims at evoking in the mind of the reader a vision, as precise and evident as possible. Think of the Proustian descriptions of the paintings by Elstir. The author, pretending to describe the work of an imaginary painter, was in fact sticking to the paintings of artists of his time.

In my novels I frequently play the game of occult ekphrasis. Such are the descriptions of two church portals (Moissac and Vezelay) and of many pages of illuminated codes in *The Name of the Rose*; such is the whole description of the nave of the Conservatoire des Arts et Métiers in *Foucault's Pendulum* (to such an extent, I hope, that now that this museum has been unfortunately refurbished, historians of the future might guess from my text how it was at the time of its lost splendour).

Let me consider two occult ekphrases from *The Island of the Day Before*: one inspired by Georges de la Tour and another inspired by Vermeer. When writing, I looked at the paintings and tried to describe them as vividly as I could. I did not mention them; I wanted the readers to believe that I was describing a real scene. This permitted me to try some little variations, so that I added or modified some details – without feeling guilty of the sin for which Steiner reproached Dante Gabriele Rossetti (who in the title of one of his poems explicitly referred to an Ingres painting and then described a considerably different scene). But I also trusted that a cultivated reader would be able to recognise my visual source and to appreciate that, if I made an ekphrasis, it was a description of a painting belonging to the same period in which my story took place – and therefore my ekphrasis was not merely a rhetorical exercise but an attempt to reconstruct the visual atmosphere of that historical moment.

Usually I signal these visual sources to my translators, but I do not ask them to translate by looking at them. I assume that, if my description is good, it should work even in another language.

However, in an occult ekphrasis one starts from the double premise that (i) if naive readers do not recognise the visual source, they can in some way discover it through their imagination, as if they were watching the scene for the first time, and that (ii) if educated readers already know the visual work, they will get an additional pleasure from the rediscovery of the work through a verbal description.

So I hope that many readers can recognise not only one, but many of Georges de la Tour's paintings, in a description like this one from chapter 31, and since Weaver's translation is absolutely correct it is not necessary to provide the original text:

> Roberto now saw Ferrante in the darkness at the mirror that reflected only the candle set before it. Contemplating two little flames, one aping the other, the eye stares, the mind is infatuated, visions rise. Shifting his head slightly, Ferrante sees Lilia, her face of virgin wax, so bathed in light that it absorbs every other ray and causes her blonde hair to flow like a dark mass wound in a spindle behind her back, her bosom just visible beneath a delicate dress, its neck cut low.

Now let us read this description from chapter 12, inspired by Vermeer:

> *Qualche sera dopo, passando davanti a una casa, la scorse in una stanza buia al piano terra. Era seduta alla finestra per cogliere un venticello che mitigava appena l'afa monferrina, fatta chiara da una lampada, invisibile dall'esterno, posata presso al davanzale. A tutta prima non l'aveva reconosciuta perché le belle chiome erano avvolte sul capo, e ne pendevano solo due ciocche sopra le orecchie. Si scorgeva solo il viso un poco chinato, un solo purissimo ovale, imperlato da qualche goccia di sudore, che pareva l'unica vera lampada in quella penombra.*
>
> *Stava lavorando di cucito su di un tavolinetto basso, su cui posava lo sguardo intento [. . .] Roberto ne vedeva il labbro, ombreggiato da una calugine bionda. A un tratto ella aveva levato una mano più luminosa ancor del viso, per portare alla bocca un filo scuro: lo aveva*

introdotto tra le labbra rosse scoprendo i denti bianchi e lo aveva reciso di un sol colpo, con mossa di fiera gentile, sorridendo lieta della sua mansueta crudeltà.

Certainly Bill Weaver's translation makes the readers visualise the image pretty well even if they are not acquainted with Vermeer's painting:

A few evenings later, passing a house, he glimpsed her in a dark room on the ground floor. To enjoy the faint breeze that barely mitigated the Monferrino sultriness, she was seated at the window, in the light of an unseen lamp placed near the sill. At first he failed to recognize her because her lovely hair was wound around her head; just two locks escaped, falling over the ears. Only her face could be seen: bent slightly, a single, pure oval beaded with a few drops of sweat, it seemed the real lamp in that penumbra.

At a little table she was occupied with some sewing, on which her intent gaze rested [. . .] Roberto noticed that her lip was shaded by blonde down. Suddenly she raised a hand even more luminous than her face, to hold a length of dark thread to her mouth placing it between her red lips, she bared her white teeth, severing it with one bite, the act of a gentle animal happily smiling in her domestic cruelty.

My only stricture is that the translator underestimated an Italian expression, to such an extent that I suspect that he was translating without having Vermeer in his mind. I say that the girl was *fatta chiara* (made clear) by an invisible lamp. Weaver translates that she was *in the light of an unseen lamp* (Jean-Noel Schifano translated that she was *éclairée par une lampe invisible*, Lozano that she was *aclarada por una lámpara*, and Kroeber says *das Gesicht im Schein einer Lampe*). They are good descriptions, but to say that one is lit up by a lamp is not the same as to say that one is made or rendered clear by a lamp: my expression transfers the source of light from the lamp to the face, and it is the girl's face which becomes the luminous source. This should be a clue for competent readers, who know that, in seventeenth-century paintings, the light radiates from faces, hands and fingers, as if the bodies themselves were alight.

Intertextual irony

Ekphrasis quotes a visual text by means of verbal texts. There is also a way to make a second verbal text visible, or detectable, though a first one. I am speaking of the procedure called *intertextual irony*. To scatter a text with non-explicit quotations of other works of art or literature is considered a form, perhaps the *typical* form, of post-modern literature – the natural effect of its intertextuality and (to invoke Bakhtin) of its dialogism, as well as a characteristic of what Hutcheon[1] calls *metafiction*. Texts always speak to each other: in every work it is possible to detect what Harold Bloom called *the anxiety of influence*. But I am speaking of intertextual irony in a more specific sense.

Intertextual irony is a strategy by which an author makes non-explicit allusions to other works, and in doing so creates a double effect: (i) naive readers, who do not understand the reference, enjoy the text as if they were receiving its message for the first time (thus, if one tells them that a character makes a thrust through an arras while shouting *a rat!*, they miss the Shakespearean echo but are nonetheless thrilled by the dramatic situation); (ii) competent readers catch the quotation, and they sense that it is ironic, especially if the quoted situation or sentence changes its sense and implies a sort of debasement. This procedure has been defined as *double coding*.

A novel or a poem can be full of quotations from the universal treasury of literature without establishing any double coding. Eliot's *The Waste Land* requires pages and pages of footnotes in order for its readers to identify explicit or implicit quotations from history, anthropology, art and so on. Eliot realised that there existed uninformed readers who would be unable to recognise his allusions and to realise how many there were and so added the footnotes as part of the poem itself. In this sense, *The Waste Land* is not a case of double coding. A reader appreciating this text only for its rhythm (for the sounds of its words, for the ghost-like literary landscape evoked by so many unknown names as Stetson, Philomel and Madame Sosostris, for quotations in German or French), is similar to a spy who eavesdrops through an open door and realises that somebody is whispering something, but lacks the indispensable code to understand what that conversation is about.

Intertextual irony has nothing to do with the fact that a text can be read at two or more levels of sense, as happened, according to the medieval hermeneutics, with the four senses of the Holy Scriptures – literal, allegorical, moral and anagogical. There are many texts that display a double level of sense: for instance parables (like the evangelical ones) and fairy tales. Certainly one can naively read the fable of the wolf and the lamb by Phaedrus as a simple report of an altercation between two animals – but to drop the moral sense of the tale would be an example of poor interpretation, and the author himself takes pains to inform his reader that *de te fabula narratur*.

We should distinguish a naive reading as an accident (due to lack of information on the part of the reader) from a naive reading programmed as legitimate by the author, even though a cultivated reading is equally admitted. Can one read the *Divine Comedy* without realising its moral purposes? A lot of romantic critics did so. Can one read the procession of the Purgatory, in the *Divine Comedy*, without taking into account its allegorical interpretation? Perhaps a surrealist poet could do so. But this has nothing to do with the post-modern poetics of double coding.

In Phaedrus's tale there are two senses (literal and moral) but no double coding. In Joyce's *Ulysses* there are two levels of sense (the story of Bloom as an allegory of the story of Ulysses), but Joyce wanted his readers to discover the double reading in some way, and the title itself is a clue. It is a waste of time to read *Finnegans Wake* and to miss its patchwork of ultraviolet allusion to the whole of human culture. The readers who read or listen to it as though they were enjoying pure music can undoubtedly be charmed by the sounds and rhythms but are not really reading what Joyce wrote.

Double coding has different purposes: it characterises a literary work which displays a lot of erudite quotations but can also attain popular success, in so far as it can be enjoyed in a naive way. To find an extreme example, take *Don Quixote* as rewritten by Pierre Menard, described by Borges in one of his stories. Menard succeeds, without copying, in reinventing Cervantes's novel word by word. According to Borges, the intelligent reader is in a position to appreciate the way in which words and sentences of Menard's text, insofar as they were written today and not centuries ago, acquire a radically different meaning from those of Cervantes – and only in this way can the irony of that imaginary rewriting be caught. However, a naive reader who has never heard of the existence of Cervantes can take the work of Menard simply as a pleasant story of a crazy knight from La Mancha.

What should translators do when facing a case like this? If by chance Menard's book existed and had to be translated, it would be mandatory to copy the most current translation of Cervantes's novel.

Thus, the practice of translation offers a good opportunity to recognise the strategy of double coding in a text: it is here that translators feel committed to find a way to make a quotation perceptible as such in their own language.

Think of the example I gave, when Diotallevi mentions a hedge. The translators had to identify the quotation and to decide that (if that quotation was opaque for a foreign reader) they ought to find a satisfying reference in their own literature. Otherwise they would have missed the point. This is a sort of commitment that translators from Phaedrus do not feel as part of their duty. The story of the wolf and the lamb has to be translated more or less literally and if readers do not catch the moral sense, too bad for them. The translator is not responsible.

As an author of novels where intertextual echoes play an important role, I am always pleased when a reader catches my allusions. *The Island of the Day Before* starts with a wink to the *Île mysterieuse* by Jules Verne (for instance, my protagonist wonders if the land he watches from his ship is an island or a continent, and one of the first subchapters of Verne's novel is entitled 'Island or continent?'). I obviously informed my translators that Roberto's question had to be phrased like Verne's, quoted exactly in the form it appeared in the best-known versions of Verne in their own language. Obviously the naive reader would be satisfied by reading that my poor shipwreck did not know anything about that mysterious land.

The problem, however, is to make translators aware of allusions that, for many reasons, might escape them. For this reason I usually send my translators pages and pages of notes about my various undetectable quotations – and suggest to them the way in which these quotations can be made perceptible in their own language. This problem was particularly urgent in *Foucault's Pendulum* since in this text the problem of double coding is squared. There it is not only the author who suggests occult quotations: there are the characters (at least Belbo, Casaubon and Diotallevi) who ironically and explicitly quote from the treasury of world literature (as we have seen in the case of the hedge).

For example, in chapter 11, one of the *files* written at the computer by Jacopo Belbo (who sets up imaginary worlds, largely intertextual, in order to overcome his neurosis at being an editor who, like Diotallevi, is unable to see life if not through literature) deals with a hero called *Jim della Canapa*. The hero's deeds are a collage of adventurous stereotypes: names of places in Polynesia or of Malaysian seas are nonchalantly mixed with those of other parts of the world where literature has situated stories of passion and death under the palm trees. My instructions to translators said that *Jim della Canapa* had to be translated by a name able to evoke the South Seas or something similar, not necessarily literally – it seemed to me that, in English, Hemp Jim would not sound right. It was not mandatory to mention hemp. Jim could have sold, instead of hemp, coconuts, and so become Coconut Jim or Seven Seas Jim. What had to be detected was that this character was a mixture of Lord Jim, Corto Maltese, Gauguin and Sanders of the River.

Thus Jim became *Jim de la Papaye* in French, *Seven Seas Jim* in English, *Jim el del Cáñam* in Spanish, curiously enough *O Tzim tes kànnabes* in Greek and, with a very beautiful reference to Kurt Weill, *Surabaya-Jim* in German.

In *The Island of the Day Before* every chapter has a title which suggests only vaguely what it is about. As a matter of fact, I feel proud to have found for every chapter the title of a seventeenth-century book. It was a *tour de force*, but a poorly paying one, since my play was understood only by a few specialists of that period and mainly by rare-book dealers and bibliophiles. Sometimes I ask myself if by chance I write novels purely in order to put in hermetic references that are comprehensible only to me. I feel like a painter who, in a landscape, puts among the leaves of the trees – almost invisible – the initials of his beloved. And it does not matter if not even she is able to identify them.

But I wanted my translators to make my play understandable in their own language. For certain books there was not only their contemporary, translated title, but also the one of their ancient original. For instance the chapter entitled *L'Arte di Prudenza* was the *Oraculo Manual y Arte de Prudencia* by Gracián. In other cases I had to resort to my knowledge as a rare-book collector and I was able to suggest analogous titles. Thus instead of *La Desiderata Scienza delle Longitudini* (written in Latin by Morin as *Longitudinum Optata Scientia*) I suggested for the English Dampier's *A New Voyage Round the World* and for the Spanish a quotation about the *Punto Fijo* from the *Dialogo de los perros* by Cervantes.

I had a beautiful Italian title, *La Nautica Rilucente* by a certain Rosa, but I realised that it was unknown and untranslatable. I suggested *Arte del Navegar* (by Medina), and *General and Rare Memorial pertaining to the perfect Art of Navigation* (by John Dee), and in German *Narrenschiff*. For *Diverse e Artificiose Macchine* by Ramelli I recommended a German translation from 1620, and for the French I proposed *Théâtre des Instruments Mathématiques et Mécaniques*, by Besson. Instead of *Teatro d'Imprese* by Ferro I picked many other emblem books such as, for instance, *Philosophie des images enigmatiques*, *Empresas Morales*, *Declaración magistral sobre los emblemas*,

Delights for the Ingenious, A Collection of Emblems, Emblematisches Lust Cabinet, Emblematische Schatz-Kammer.

Another piece of instruction I gave was that the whole travel of *Amarilli* was a collage of intertextual allusion to famous persons and islands. Mas Afuera was the island of the Juan Fernandez archipelago where Robinson Crusoe (the historical one, that is, Selkirk) was shipwrecked. The unnamed island where they arrived after the Galapagos was Pitcairn, and the *Bounty* Mutiny was evoked there. The next island was Gaugin's one. When the knight reaches an island where he tells the natives fascinating stories and they call him Tusitala, there is a clear mention of Stevenson. When the knight suggests Roberto slide into the sea (*at that moment we would know everything*), there is a direct quotation from Martin Eden's suicide. The sentence by Roberto, *ma appena lo sapessimo, cesseremmo di saperlo*, is a quotation from the first Italian translation of the last sentence of Jack London's novel (*and at the instant he knew, he ceased to know*). Obviously Bill Weaver got the allusion and translated 'Yes, but at the instant we knew it, we would cease to know.'

When a text is based on double coding, however, the possibility of a double reading depends on the size of the encyclopaedia of the reader. When playing dialogism, it is difficult to resist the fascination of intertextual reverberations. Linda Hutcheon[2] finds on page 378 of the English version of my *Pendulum*: 'The Rule is simple: Suspect, only suspect', and identifies a clear quotation: *Connect, only connect*, from E. M. Forster. She is prudent enough to observe that this 'ironic play' appears in the English version. As a matter of fact the Italian original text (and I do not know if Hutcheon had it in front of her when making this remark) does not display such an intertextual connection, because it reads *sospettare, sospettare sempre* (suspect, always suspect). The explicit reference has been introduced by the translator – consciously, I suspect. This demonstrates how every translation can either weaken or reinforce a strategy of double coding.

At one stage in chapter 30 of the *Pendulum*, my protagonists get lost in reverie and think that the whole story told by the Gospels could be the effect of an invention, like the Universal Plot he and his friends are concocting. Since a fake Gospel is by definition apocryphal, Causaubon sophomorically comments: *Toi, apochryphe lecteur, mon semblable, mon frère.* When writing I would have been satisfied if the reader caught the reference to Baudelaire (*toi, hypocrite lecteur . . .*), but Linda Hutcheon sees my quotation as a 'parody of Baudelaire by Eliot' (in fact, Eliot quotes Baudelaire in *The Waste Land*). This way my game becomes wittier than it was intended to be. Fortunately, if Hutcheon had translated my book, her astute interpretation could not have changed the translation (it was obviously mandatory to keep the quotation in French). In any case Hutcheon's suggestion posits a nice problem for the poetics of double coding. Should we split the readers between those whose encyclopaedia includes only Baudelaire and those who are also conscious of the Eliot–Baudelaire relationship? And what to say about possible readers who found the quotation in Eliot, ignoring that it was referring back to Baudelaire? Should we deny them the membership in the club of intertextuality?

In *The Island of the Day Before* there are some *coups de théâtre* in Dumas's style. I was ready also to accept readers unable to identify the quotations and eager to enjoy certain situations for their cloak-and-dagger flavour, irrespective of the source. In chapter 17, when Mazarin dismisses Roberto de la Grive after having entrusted him with a secret mission, the voice of the Narrator says:

Piegò un ginocchio e disse: 'Eminenza, sono vostro.'

    O almeno così vorrei, visto che non mi pare costumato fargli dare un salvacondotto che reciti 'C'est par mon ordre et pour le bien de l'état que le porteur du présent a fait ce qu'il a fait.'

The English translation reads:

He bent one knee, and said: 'Eminence, I am yours.'

    Or at least that is what I would have liked to happen, for it does not seem to me civil to give him a safe-conduct that says, 'C'est par mon ordre et pour le bien de l'état que le porteur du présent a fait ce qu'il a fait.'

Bill Weaver identified the quotation, respected it and, to make it recognisable as a quotation, followed me and left it in French. Respect for double coding overcame need for literal comprehensibility.

It is interesting to notice that Weaver's solution has been adopted by the translators in Slovak, Finnish, Swedish, Romanian, Czech, Serbian, Polish, Turkish, Spanish, Portuguese (in both the Portuguese and Brazilian versions), Catalan, Danish, Dutch, Latvian, Norwegian and Greek. But the Russian, German, Chinese, Japanese, Macedonian and Hungarian translators put the quotation in their own language. In the German case I would say that Kroeber was sure that the original text would be recognised in any case, because there are many German translations of Dumas. Probably Chinese and Japanese translators were not sure that their readers could identify such a culturally remote source (I do not know, it may also be that Dumas is so well known in Japan that every Japanese reader can find the right track). Perhaps they found it disturbing to insert a quotation in Latin characters. But it seems to me that problems of alphabet are scarcely relevant, otherwise Serbian and Greek versions would not have used the original quotation.

I think that in each of the above cases the translator has *negotiated*, deciding whether it was more convenient to miss the intertextual link for the sake of comprehensibility or whether on the contrary it was necessary to risk a poor literal understanding in order to stress the link.

Note that there is a double textual play in this short passage. First, the intrusion of the Narrator who apologises for having avoided the quotation of a famous line (a case of *praeterition* or *paraleipsis*, since while apologising for non-quoting in fact he quotes). Second, the textual quotation of the safe-conduct that Richelieu gives Milady, Athos purloins from her and at the end d'Artagnan shows to Richelieu. Here naive readers seem to be left without any help. They understand that Mazarin *did not give* Roberto a safe-conduct (if they do not know French they ignore what it is about), and worry about why the Narrator feels compelled to say that something irrelevant *did not happen*. But, since the quotation is in another language, they are in some way pulled to suspect that there is a quotation.[3]

So much for double coding. Once again it is a case where translation is not only a linguistic but also, or mainly, a cultural affair.

NOTES

1. Hutcheon, Linda, *A Poetics of Postmodernism* (London: Routledge, 1988), chapter 7.
2. 'Eco's echoes: ironizing the (post)modern', in N. Bourchard and V. Pravadelli, eds., *Umberto Eco's Alternative. The Politics of Culture and the Ambiguities of Interpretation* (New York: Peter Lang, 1998), p. 166.
3. In at least two English translations I consulted, the safe-conduct reads 'It is by my order that the bearer of this paper has done what he has just done,' a version which contains two mistakes. First, it does not translate that all this happened for the State's sake, and second this translation uses the masculine pronoun *he*, while the French original remains uncommitted. So it remains difficult to understand how a safe-conduct given to Milady could have been used by d'Artagnan, or why (vices of an old-fashioned sexism) a letter given a woman should use the pronoun *he*.

SIX

From rewording to translating substance

If in order to translate one must make a series of hypotheses about the deep sense and the purposes of a text, then translation is certainly a form of interpretation – at least insofar as it depends on a series of previous interpretations. However, to say that translation is a form of interpretation does not imply that interpretation is a form of translation. No logically educated mind would say so.

Here I feel embarrassed, because I have to criticise one of the scholars I have most admired in my life, and whom I still consider a master and an unforgettable friend – the late Roman Jakobson. But Jakobson was once responsible for a possible confusion.

Translation and interpretation

In his essay on the linguistic aspects of translation, Jakobson[1] (1959) suggested that there are three types of translation: *intralinguistic*, *interlinguistic* and *intersemiotic*.

Intralinguistic translation, or 'rewording', is 'an interpretation of verbal signs by means of other signs of the same language'.

Interlinguistic translation is when a text is translated from one language to another, in other words when we have 'an interpretation of verbal signs by means of signs of some other language' (which is translation proper).

Intersemiotic translation or transmutation is when we have 'an interpretation of verbal signs by means of signs of non-verbal systems', for example, when a novel is 'translated' into a film, or a fairy tale into a ballet. Jakobson did not quote cases like Walt Disney's *Fantasia*, where music is translated into images.

In order to define the three types of translation, Jakobson uses the word *interpretation* three times, and it could not be otherwise for a linguist who, while belonging to the structuralist tradition, was the first to discover the fecundity of Peircean concepts. However, his definition of the three types of translation leaves us with an ambiguity. The first way to read this classification is that there are three types of interpretation, and that in this sense translation is a species of the genus *interpretation*. This seems the most obvious solution, and the fact that Jakobson insisted on the term *translation* could have been due to the fact that he wrote down his reflections for a collection of essays devoted to the problem of translation, in which his aim was to distinguish between various types of translation, implicitly taking for granted that they were all forms of interpretation. But, on the grounds of Jakobson's proposal, many people decided that he was suggesting that rewording, translation proper and transmutation were three types of translation:

	rewording
Translation	translation proper
	transmutation

Since, as we shall see, the category of *rewording* covers an immense variety of types of interpretation, at this point it would be easy to succumb to the temptation to identify the totality of semiosis with a continuous process of translation – in other words, to assert that every interpretation is a form of translation.

Such an idea has at times been supported by various hermeneutical philosophers. Heidegger, during a university course on Heraclitus in 1943, proclaimed the identity between translation and interpretation.[2] Gadamer[3] maintained on the one hand that 'every translation is always an interpretation', in the sense that a translation is made possible by a previous interpretation of a text – and this cannot be reasonably refuted – but on the other hand he tried to show the deep structural identity between the two, in the sense that translating is like performing a dialogue with Another One, and in every dialogue one tries to understand the point of view of the interlocutor.

Gadamer states that every translator is an interpreter, and I agree, but this does not mean that every interpreter is a translator. In another place he says that the task of the translator is not qualitatively different from the one of an interpreter, but differs only in the degree of intensity. Such a difference in degrees of intensity seems to me fundamental, and in the course of this chapter I shall distinguish those different degrees.

George Steiner[4] says that

A 'theory' of translation, a 'theory' of semantic transfer, must mean one of two things. It is either an intentionally sharpened, hermeneutically oriented way of designating a working model of *all* meaningful exchanges, of the totality of semantic communication (including Jakobson's intersemiotic translation or 'transmutation'). Or it is a subsection of such a model with specific reference to interlingual exchanges, to the emission and reception of significant messages between different languages.

Steiner adds that 'the "totalising" designation is the more instructive because it argues the fact that all procedures of expressive articulation and interpretative reception are translational, whether intra- or interlingually. The second usage – "translation involves two or more languages" – has the advantage of obviousness and common currency; but it is, I believe, damagingly restrictive.'

Steiner honestly admits that both the totalising and the traditionally specific theory can be used with systematic adequacy only if they relate to a given theory of language. One has to decide whether 'a theory of translation is in fact a theory of language' or whether 'the theory of language is the whole of which the theory of translation is a part'. He says that 'the preceding chapters have made my own preference clear'.

It is clear that my preferences are different, because my own theory of language is based upon Peirce's notion of interpretation, a notion which is too large to be reduced to the one of translation.

Many forms of interpretation

According to Peirce an expression (be it linguistic or not) can be interpreted by a synonym, a definition, a paraphrase, a series of inferences or even by a series of encyclopaedic explanations. For instance, let us take the expression *cocaine*. It can be interpreted by a synonym, and as far as I know it is called *coke*, *snow*, and many other slang expressions. *Cocaine* can be interpreted by a definition, and I found in *Webster's* 'white crystalline alkaloid extracted from coca leaves'. But the same dictionary also provides an inference, when saying that this substance 'can produce addiction'. If by chance someone didn't understand all these interpretations, I could add some encyclopaedic details, such as, let us say, that some natives in Latin America used to chew those leaves, or that Sherlock Holmes took such a substance in a seven-per-cent solution.

Peirce said that the interpretant is something that teaches us something more about the interpreted sign. If I interpret *cocaine* as 'crystalline alkaloid' I know certain properties of cocaine that I probably did not know before. But this 'more' might be 'less' as far as the sense of a given discourse was concerned.

For instance, according to Peirce, the interpretant of a given expression can also be a behavioural or an emotional response (Peirce was speaking of an *energetic interpretant*). Now, suppose that I am following a play in a language I do not know well enough. When an actor utters something, I notice that the other people on stage (and probably also people in the audience) are laughing, so I infer that the actor said something funny. These laughs act as an interpretant of the first actor's utterance, telling me that he told a joke; but they do not tell me what the joke was about.

Not only this, I cannot tell whether it was a witty quip or trivial wordplay. In my ignorance I do not understand why the other actors laugh. They may be laughing because they are so simple-minded as to appreciate a vulgar prankster, or so quick as to love the boldest of paradoxes. This *Gedankenexperiment* tells us that something can act as an interpretant of a given expression without being a translation of it – at least in the proper sense of the word.

Rewording is not translation

Jakobson spoke of translation also as rewording. Now let us suppose that the most elementary case of rewording, that is, definition, can be taken as a translation. Since in chapter 2 I quoted the scene where Hamlet kills Polonius, let me return to that text:

GERTRUDE What wilt thou do? thou wilt not murder me? Help, help, ho!

POLONIUS (*Behind*) What, ho! help, help, help!

HAMLET (*Drawing*) How now! a rat? Dead, for a ducat, dead!

Makes a pass through the arras

POLONIUS (*Behind*) O, I am slain!

Falls and dies

If I look in *Webster's* for correct definitions of the main terms used by Shakespeare I find:

Do – to make or cause, to perform or carry out

Murder – to kill unlawfully and with malice

Help – aid or assistance

Behind – on the side opposite to front

Draw – to pull out, to remove, to extract, as a cork, a tooth, a sword

Rat – any of several kinds of black, brown or grey, long-tailed rodents, resembling, but larger than, the mouse

Dead – no longer living

Ducat – any of various coins of silver formerly current in Europe

Arras – a tapestry

Slay – to kill by violence

Fall – to come down by the force of gravity
Die – to cease to live, to come to an end

Consequently the passage could be reworded as:

GERTRUDE What wilt thou make or cause, to perform or carry out? thou wilt not kill me unlawfully and with malice? Assistance, assistance, ho!
POLONIUS (*on the side opposite to front*) What, ho! Assistance! Assistance! Assistance!
HAMLET (*pulling out, removing, extracting, as a cork, a tooth, a sword*) How now! Any of several kinds of black, brown or grey, long-tailed rodents, resembling, but larger than, the mouse? No longer living, for a coin of silver, no longer living!
Makes a pass through the tapestry
POLONIUS (*on the side opposite to front*) O, I am killed by violence!
Comes down by the force of gravity and comes to an end

It's a joke, I agree. But this joke has been made possible by having identified translation with interpretation through definition, that is, by having rigorously (mechanically) respected the (evidently absurd) principle that definition – insofar as it is a form of rewording – is a form of translation. It goes without saying that this text would not be a correct translation even if it were literally translated into another language.

Synonyms are a form of rewording. With the help of *Roget's Thesaurus* I can rephrase our Shakespearean text, to obtain something that no publisher would pay for as a translation:

GERTRUDE What wilt thou cook? thou wilt not remove me from life? Do a favour, do a favour, ho!
POLONIUS (*Back to back*) What, ho! Do a favour, do a favour, do a favour!
HAMLET (*Phlebotomising*) How now! a bad person? Deceased, for a napoleon, deceased!

Makes a stab through the tapestry
POLONIUS (*Back to back*) O, I am put out of the way!
Descends and is burned out.

Paraphrase is certainly a form of rewording. My late friend Guido Almansi, who also taught in Great Britain for a long time, once published, along with Guido Fink, an anthology of parodies.[5] One of the chapters of that amusing collection of masterpieces was entitled 'Il falso innocente' (*The innocent fake*) and concerned unconscious parodies – that is, versions of great works *ad usum Delphini* which represent a form of interpretation by summary. One of the most preposterous examples of paraphrase was given by the *Tales from Shakespeare* written at the beginning of the nineteenth century by Charles and Mary Lamb. Let me quote only a few passages concerning *Hamlet.*

Hamlet's madness was love. And the queen wished that the good beauties of Ophelia might be the happy cause of his wildness, for so she hoped that her virtues might happily restore him to his accustomed way again [. . .] But Hamlet's malady lay deeper than she supposed, or than could be so cured [. . .] His very melancholy, and the dejection of spirits he had so long been in, produced an irresoluteness and wavering of purpose which kept him from proceeding to extremities.

Coming to our scene, there is the undoubtedly clarifying paraphrase:

Said the queen, 'if you show me so little respect, I will set those to you that can speak,' and was going to send the king or Polonius to him. But Hamlet would not let her go, now he had her alone, till he had tried if his words could not bring her to some sense of her wicked life; and, taking her by the wrist, he held her fast, and made her sit down. She, affrighted at his earnest manner, and fearful lest in his lunacy he should do her a mischief, cried out; and a voice was heard from behind the hangings, 'Help, help, the queen!' which Hamlet hearing, and verily thinking that it was the king himself there concealed, he drew his sword and stabbed at the place where the voice came from, as he would have stabbed a rat that ran there, till the voice ceasing, he concluded the person to be dead. But when he dragged forth the body, it was not the king, but Polonius, the old officious counsellor, that had planted himself as a spy behind the hangings. 'Oh me!' exclaimed the queen, 'what a rash and bloody deed have you done!' 'A bloody deed, mother,' replied Hamlet, 'but not so bad as yours, who killed a king, and married his brother.'

Is that a good translation from Shakespeare? I suspect it is not. But let us go on. We have said that even a comment which draws inferences from a text is a form of interpretation. In the milieu of the French Oulipo it was suggested that the opening line of *À la recherche* by Proust, *Longtemps je me suis couché de bonne heure*, could be interpreted by the following inference: *It took me a long time to convince my parents to let me go to bed after nine.* This is certainly another excellent example of interpretation which is certainly not a good example of translation.

Now, what do all these cases of rewording have in common? Each of them tried to communicate the same content as the original, but with different words. This means that in order to render the same content the interpretation has to change the form of the expression, or the discourse – in the sense that, linguistically speaking, the definitions *felis catus* or *animal which miaows* are linguistic strings different from *cat*. Can we say that even translation proper does the same? From a certain point of view it does, since nobody can deny that if I translate the passage from *Hamlet* into Italian the linguistic strings would be different. However, why can *come? un topo!* be considered a correct translation of *how now! a rat!* when we consider a translation like *How now? Any of several kinds of black, brown or grey, long-tailed rodents, resembling, but larger than, the mouse!* to be a joke?

Reformulations in other semiotic systems

We must first of all consider the fact that under the headings of what Jakobson called rewording (intended as the *reformulation* of a given expression within the same semiotic system) one should also put cases of reformulation in a non-verbal system. In music such a procedure is usually called transcription, as when a musical piece is rewritten in a different key, or changed from major to minor or (in ancient times) from the Dorian mode to the Phrygian mode. In these cases it seems there is no change in substance (we are always using sounds, perhaps produced by the same instrument) and both the melodic line and the harmonic relationship are preserved. But there are cases in which a given composition is transcribed for a different instrument. Take for instance Bach's Solo Cello Suites transcribed for alto recorder. The change in the substance of the expression is at this point relevant, even for an absent-minded listener. First of all, it is true that the melodic line is transported point by point from one instrument to the other, without variations, but the same does not happen with the chords. The bow of the cello can be drawn across more than one string at the same time, while with a recorder one can play no more than one note at a time. The solution is 'to translate' a given chord into an *arpeggio*: the soloist plays several notes one after the other very rapidly so to create the aural impression of performing all of them at the same instant.

Second, there is a shift from a given timbre to another, and this feature is certainly perceived even by the most inattentive listener. Both from the melodic and harmonic point of view the transcription should allow everybody to recognise the original score, but such identification is not as easy as it seems. I play the Solo Cello Suites on the alto recorder, and even though I am a very modest performer I could say I know them by heart. In spite of this, it has happened many times (while doing something else) that I have listened absently to a melody played by a cello on the radio, and have the impression of knowing it but am unable to immediately identify it. It took a certain effort to realise that it was one of those suites I knew so well. Changing the timbre meant that the effect of the piece was a different one. Thus we can say that a mutation in substance has a consistent impact on the listener.

Can we say that this does not happen with verbal languages?

Substance in rewording

In chapter 1 I wrote that at the expression level of a text there is not just one single substance at play. There is the properly linguistic substance, but it is conveyed and supported by many suprasegmental elements such as tone of voice, pitch, the rhythm and speed of the utterance and so on. All these features of an expressed substance do not have anything to do with the language as a system. Accent is for instance a substance phenomenon but, in respect of the form of a language, is considered a suprasegmental business – in other words, an Australian worker pronounces the sentence *There is a pot on the table* differently from an Oxford professor, but this has nothing to do with English grammar and both the uttered sentences can be paraphrased or translated in the same way. Thus in every new utterance of the same sentence there is a change in substance in the sense that the same expression uttered by two different persons displays two different tones of voice.

Differences in timbre are still linguistic features (Hjelsmlev called them *connotators*) but are relevant only when we want to recognise someone who is speaking out of sight. They are mainly used as *clues* in order to identify things or individuals. From the point of view of the sense of the expression, or of the content substance, these features are irrelevant, and the same happens with all cases of rewording such as definitions, summaries, comments, inferential developments. In these cases we are interested in grasping what an expression means, and the physical way such a meaning is conveyed does not interest us.

The same seems to happen with variations in graphic substances. Suppose I produce a written expression and then I reproduce it on this page many times:

Mothers love their children
Mothers love their children
Mothers love their children
Mothers love their children
Mothers love their children

In these five cases we have the same Linear Manifestation, and the physical variations of the five strings are irrelevant (only through a microscope could one detect infinitesimal differences in the printing). Thus I have repeated the same written sentence five times. But now let's suppose I reproduce the same sentence in three different fonts:

Mothers love their children

Mothers love their children

Mothers love their children

A font is a particular 'form' but this change in the form of the graphic expression also represents a change in substance, since different fonts produce different visual reactions. Might we say that these three sentences act on our senses as if they were pronounced respectively by a cockney woman, by an Eton student and by an old Highland shepherd? I think that there is something more: in the graphic case we shold also appreciate the aesthetic aim of the printer, to such an extent that if we consider a pseudo-futurist line like

Explosiooone! Una booOmba!

in an English translation we should also keep the graphic substance as a relevant feature of the poem, thus translating:

Explooosion! A booOOmb!

The same would happen if the sentence were uttered in the course of a comedy. Then the differences between the accents of a cockney woman, an Eton student and an old Highland shepherd would become relevant (to the extent that if the Highland shepherd spoke with an Eton accent, the effect would be comic). This means that in certain texts, intended to produce an aesthetic or poetic effect, differences in substance become highly relevant.

I think that something similar happens when – in translation of verbal texts from one language to another – one tries to produce the same effect with two different substances of expression.

In cases of rewording, like definition or paraphrase or inference, where the content is interpreted in a more detailed way, we can say that:

$$LS_1/C_1 \rightarrow LS_2/C_{1a} \text{ where } C_{1a} > C_1$$

A Linguistic Substance$_1$ that conveys a Content$_1$ is transformed into a Linguistic Substance$_2$ that conveys a Content$_{1a}$ where Content$_{1a}$ is $>$ than Content$_1$ (and I use $>$ not in a strictly logical sense but as shorthand in order to say 'the same content but more detailed', as when I defined cocaine as an alkaloid).

Substance in translation

In elementary processes of translation (for instance, by satisfactorily translating *I am eating a piece of bread* as *Sto mangiando un pezzo di pane* or *Je suis en train de manger un morceau de pain*) a Linguistic Substance$_1$ that conveys a Content$_1$ is transformed into a Linguistic Substance$_2$ that aims at conveying the same Content$_1$

$$LS_1/C_1 \rightarrow LS_2/C_1$$

Usually we are not overly interested in the fact that a Substance$_1$ is transformed into a Substance$_2$ because in cases of elementary translation (as in rewording) we are mainly interested in grasping the content. But we have felt disturbed when we have tried to translate a few lines from *Hamlet* into definitions and paraphrases. This means that for certain texts there are many stylistic features such as, for instance, metre, or the sound of words, or the brevity of an exchange, that are independent from the structure of a given language (a hendecasyllable displays the same features both in English and in Italian) and which must be respected by a translation.

I have suggested that these texts are those that we consider as endowed with aesthetic qualities. However, let us take a step backwards. Is it certain that changes in substance are absolutely irrelevant as far as non-poetic, trivial and everyday expressions are concerned? We have seen in one of my previous essays that even when translating the French expression *mon petit chou* we feel that we should preserve certain qualities of the uttered substance of the expression, but this requirement holds even for the most utilitarian expressions.

We know that when an English text is translated into French or Italian or German it becomes a little longer, even if the translator is able to keep the same number of words, because English certainly has more monosyllabic words than, let us say, German. Italian words are very long but less so than many German ones, while German uses fewer words than Italian or French because it can resort to many compounds. Such differences can be qualified to such an extent that typographers and publishers are able to calculate how to compose parallel texts in different languages.

Let me consider the first paragraph of the second page of the *User's Guide to the musical instrument Casio CTK-671*. The English text reads:

384 tones, including 1000 'Advanced Tones'.

A total of 238 standard tones, including piano, organ, brass, and other presets provide you with the sounds you need, while memory for 10 user tones lets you store your own original creations. 100 of the present tones are 'Advanced Tones', which are variations of standard tones created by programming in effects (DSP) and other settings.

Three versions, Italian, French and German follow. In this table I registered first the number of words and then the printed lines for every language:

English	French	Italian	German
62/5	63/6	64/6	60/7

It is evident that the English text is the shortest, that the German one uses fewer but longer words, and that the Italian text is a little longer than the French one. Considering all the lines of the whole of the second page, the results are:

English	French	Italian	German
27	30	31	34

– which means that the French, Italian and German texts shift to page 3. With unimportant variations, more or less the same ratio is respected in the following pages of the manual. If by chance the German text were sixty lines long, a typographer who did not know German might assume that it was not a translation but rather a paraphrase of the English one.

Probably nobody would protest if the Italian instructions for the Casio CTK-671 were three pages longer than the English. However, although it is admitted that in translation proper the substance of the expression changes – since we are shifting from the sounds of one language to the sounds of another – even in the most practical cases there is a sort of implicit stricture by which a certain *ratio* between substances must be respected.

This encourages me to say that *every translation proper has an aesthetic or poetic aspect.* If to interpret always means to respect the spirit (allow me this metaphor) of a text, to translate means to respect also its body.[6]

Naturally this duty of respect becomes mandatory in every text with an aesthetic aim. But we can say that, from the translation of the Casio manual to the translation of Shakespeare's sonnets, there is a continuum of possibilities of respecting the substance.

Substance in translating poetry

Now, it is universally acknowledged that in translating poetry one should render as much as possible the effect produced by the sounds of the original text, even though in the change of language a lot of variations are unavoidable. One can miss the real *body* of a discourse, but try at least to preserve, let us say, rhythm and rhyme.

So in these kinds of translation we have a process of this kind:

$$LS_1 ES_1 \; / \; C_1 \; \rightarrow \; LS_{1a} \; ES_{1a} \; / \; C_{1a}$$

where not only a Linguistic Substance$_1$ but also many Extra-Linguistic Substances$_1$ conveying a Content$_1$ are transformed into a Linguistic Substance$_{1a}$ and Extra-Linguistic Substances$_{1a}$ supposed to be aesthetically equivalent to the source ones, and conveying a Content$_{1a}$ aesthetically equivalent to the source one.

What does aesthetically equivalent mean?

In his beautiful book *Le Ton beau de Marot*[7] Douglas Hofstadter considers different translations from Dante Alighieri's *Divine Comedy*, starting from the principle that the most important stylistic and metrical feature of that poem is the invention of the tercet – that is, strophes of three verses each, all in hendecasyllables, and with the rhyme-scheme ABA, BCB, CDC and so on. Hofstadter, to stress the quasi-musical structure of a series of tercets, provides this graphic representation:

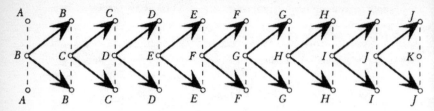

The abstract pattern of Dante's terza rima, with each tercet, or terzina, symbolized by a vertical dashed line segment.

It's evident that such a form is independent of any natural language and can be embodied in different linguistic substances. Hofstadter takes the opening tercets of the Canto Terzo:

PER ME SI VA NE LA CITTÀ DOLENTE,
PER ME SI VA NE L'ETTERNO DOLORE,
PER ME SI VA TRA LA PERDUTA GENTE.

GIUSTIZIA MOSSE IL MIO ALTO FATTORE:
FECEMI LA DIVINA PODESTATE,
LA SOMMA SAPIENZA E 'L PRIMO AMORE.

DINANZI A ME NON FUOR COSE CREATE
SE NON ETTERNE, E IO ETTERNO DURO.
LASCIATE OGNE SPERANZA, VOI CH'INTRATE.

Queste parole di colore oscuro
vid'io scritte al sommo d'una porta;
per ch'io: «Maestro, il senso lor m'è duro»

and starts examining some English translations of these verses. For instance Robert Pinsky[8] renders them:

THROUGH ME YOU ENTER INTO THE CITY OF WOES,
THROUGH ME YOU ENTER INTO ETERNAL PAIN,
THROUGH ME YOU ENTER THE POPULATION OF LOSS.

JUSTICE MOVED MY HIGHER MAKER, IN POWER DIVINE,
WISDOM SUPREME, LOVE PRIMAL. NO THINGS WERE
BEFORE ME NOT ETERNAL; ETERNAL I REMAIN.

ABANDON ALL HOPE, YE WHO ENTER HERE.
These words I saw inscribed in some dark color
Over a portal. 'Master', I said, 'make clear

Their meaning, which I find too hard to gather.'
Then he, as one who understands: 'All fear
Must be left here, and cowardice die. Together . . .

Hofstadter comments: 'It pains me to break things off so abruptly here, especially to leave unclosed the pair of quotation marks opened near the bottom, but what can I do? After all, Pinsky chose to redistribute Dante's semantics quite radically across tercets. Indeed, in this canto Dante has forty-five tercets, Pinsky has but thirty-seven. The aesthetics of this decision boggles my mind' (p. 533).

In a collection of translations edited by Daniel Halpern[9] Hofstadter picks up the translation by the great Irish poet Seamus Heaney:

THROUGH ME IT LEADS TO THE CITY SORROWFUL.
THROUGH ME IT LEADS TO THE ETERNAL PAIN.
THROUGH ME IT LEADS AMONG THE LOST PEOPLE.

JUSTICE INSPIRED MY MAKER ABOVE.
IT WAS DIVINE POWER THAT FORMED ME,
SUPREME WISDOM AND ORIGINAL LOVE.

BEFORE ME NO THING WAS CREATED EXCEPT THINGS
EVERLASTING. AND I AM EVERLASTING.
LEAVE EVERY HOPE BEHIND YOU, YOU WHO ENTER.

I saw these words inscribed above a gate
in obscure characters, and so I said,
'Master, I find their sense hard to interpret.'

Hofstadter complains first of all that Heaney does not preserve either the metre or the rhyme, but is very severe also on many other counts:

> In favour of Heaney, I can say that he renders a tercet by a tercet. It's good to see nine lines of gate inscription, instead of just seven. But, I regret to say, there's not much more praise that I can offer. Look at the first line: 'Through me it leads to the city sorrowful.' 'It'?! What is this 'it'? And 'city sorrowful' is pretty sorrowful. If this line had been written by a high-school student, I would have struck it out in bright red ink and said to start again from scratch. To my ear, the sentence doesn't even sound like it was written by a native speaker! (p. 535).

Then Hofstadter considers a translation by Mark Musa,[10] who did not use rhymes, claiming: 'My main reason for avoiding rhyme has been the results achieved by all those who have used rhyme in translating *The Divine Comedy*: they have shown that the price paid was disastrously high. I believe that all those who have offered rhymed translations of Dante could have produced far better poems if they had not used rhyme.'

> I AM THE WAY INTO THE DOLEFUL CITY,
> I AM THE WAY INTO ETERNAL GRIEF,
> I AM THE WAY TO A FORSAKEN RACE.
>
> JUSTICE IT WAS THAT MOVED MY GREAT CREATOR;
> DIVINE OMNIPOTENCE CREATED ME,
> AND HIGHEST WISDOM JOINED WITH PRIMAL LOVE.
>
> BEFORE ME NOTHING BUT ETERNAL THINGS
> WERE MADE, AND I SHALL LAST ETERNALLY.
> ABANDON EVERY HOPE, ALL YOU WHO ENTER.
>
> I saw these words spelled out in somber colors
> inscribed along the ledge above a gate;
> 'Master,' I said, 'these words I see are cruel.'

Hofstadter observes that 'although it does not rhyme at all, I find it of far greater appeal than the preceding two, firstly because it does not show any evidence of having been a struggle (though it no doubt was), and secondly because it comes far closer to mirroring the precision of Dante's meter' (pp. 536–7).

It is curious that Hofstadter does not consider the translation of Dorothy L. Sayers[11] (1949) that, in my opinion, does the best in at least partly preserving the hendecasyllables and the rhyme:

> THROUGH ME THE ROAD TO THE CITY OF DESOLATION,
> THROUGH ME THE ROAD TO SORROWS DIUTURNAL,
> THROUGH ME THE ROAD AMONG THE LOST CREATION.
>
> JUSTICE MOVED MY GREAT MAKER; GOD ETERNAL
> WROUGHT ME: THE POWER, AND THE UNSEARCHABLY
> HIGH WISDOM, AND THE PRIMAL LOVE SUPERNAL.
>
> NOTHING ERE I WAS MADE TO BE
> SAVE THINGS ETERNE, AND I ETERNE ABIDE;
> LAY DOWN ALL HOPE, YOU THAT GO IN BY ME.
>
> These words, of sombre colour, I descried
> Writ on the lintel of a gateway; 'Sir,
> This sentence is right hard for me,' I cried.

However, sometimes to respect the rhyme is not enough to produce an equivalent effect.

In Eliot's 'The Love Song of J. Alfred Prufrock' there are the famous two lines:

> In the room the women come and go
> Talking of Michelangelo.

There is, if not a rhyme, an assonance, and Italian translations (both by Luigi Berti and Roberto Sanesi)[12] did not respect it (by the way, they translate the whole poem without rhyme):

Nella stanza le donne vanno e vengono
Parlando di Michelangelo.

In the French translation,[13] Pierre Leyris attempts to maintain an effect of rhyme by changing the meaning of the source expression:

Dans la pièce les femmes vont et viennent
En parlant des maîtres de Sienne.

A recent Italian translation,[14] rather clumsily, has a false rhyme and a bad assonance:

Le donne vanno e vengono nei salotti
Parlando di Michelangelo Buonarroti.

This is one of those cases in which the translator feels entitled to change the reference of the source text in order to preserve its effect. But is there a real preservation of the effect? Even though the rhyme has been saved, we have lost the wit of the original assonance, which also presupposes an English accent in the pronunciation of the Italian name (not *Michelan'gelo* but *Michelangelo'*), and thus acquires a debasing effect. Moreover, speaking of the Masters of Siena (let alone knowing the family name of Michelangelo) presupposes some competence in the history of Italian painting, while 'Michelangelo' is popular and available enough for a kitsch usage. I suspect that these ladies speaking of Michelangelo appear more *bas bleu* or blue-stocking than if they were speaking of Duccio di Buoninsegna or Simone Martini. At this point I decide that a rhymeless solution is better than a rhymed one. However, neither Berti nor Sanesi were insensitive to other problems of substance: the nine syllables of Eliot's first line and the eight of the second became in Italian, respectively, a dodecasyllable and a nine-syllable line. The distich thus keeps a sort of lapidary gnomic dignity.

As a matter of fact the original 'Prufrock' is entirely rhymed (*Let us go then, you and I, / When the evening is spread out against the sky /*

Like a patient etherised upon a table; / Let us go, through certain half-deserted streets, / The muttering retreats ... and so on). The Italian translations are not. Was it a case of mere laziness? Once I tried to retranslate part of the poem finding acceptable rhymes, and I quote only a few lines for reasons of humility, to show to what an extent I consider my attempt unsuccessful: *Tu ed io, è già l'ora, andiamo nella sera / che nel cielo si spande in ombra nera / come un malato già in anestesia. / Andiam per certe strade desolate / nel brusio polveroso / di certi alberghi ad ore, in cui folate / senti di notti insonni, e l'acre odore / di ristoranti pregni di sudore* ...

I stopped because I had the impression of having written an Italian poem of the late nineteenth century. *My* Eliot sounds too similar to certain verses published by the Italian poet Lorenzo Stecchetti in 1877 (*Sbadigliando languir solo e soletto – Lunghi e tedosi giorni, – Dormire e ricader disteso in letto – Finchè il lsonno ritorni, – Sentir la mente e il core in etisia, – Ecco la vita mia*).

Perhaps my translation would have been acceptable to Italian readers if published in 1911 (when 'Prufrock' was written), but Berti's translation is from the 1940s and Sanesi's from the early 1960s. At that time Italian culture was receiving Eliot as a very contemporary poet and was reading him after having read the Italian experimental poets like the Hermetics. In this sense Eliot had a great influence on the further Italian neo-avant-garde. Italian readers enjoyed a certain dryness in Eliot, a quasi-prosaic style, as a reaction against a lot of traditional poetry. We are here facing the phenomenon of the so-called *horizon of the translator.*[15] Each translation is received within the framework (or 'the horizon') of literary conventions that inevitably influence the choices of the translator. Berti and Sanesi were moving in the Italian literary horizon of the mid-twentieth century and did not avoid rhyme out of laziness, but because they negotiated their version by taking into account the expectations of the Italian readers of their times. They decided that the rhyme, in Eliot, was less important than the representation of a 'waste' land and that it was of primary importance to save the reference to *sawdust restaurants* full of *oyster-shells* (that, by the way, recalled Montale's *Ossi di seppia*, bones of cuttlefish for the Italian reader). To render rhymes at any cost risked making Eliot too 'gentle' and operatic, thus losing the feeling of that 'handful of dust' that pervades so many of his poems.

Italian translations of 'Prufrock' were thus determined by the historical moment at which they were made and by the 'translator's horizon'. This is the reason why translations, in general, age.

I do not want to spend any more words on the difficulty of translating poetry, nor to consider the many theories of how poetry is untranslatable and can only inspire imitation, rewriting, and so on. I want only to stress that poetic texts are a sort of touchstone for translation, because they make clear that a translation can be considered absolutely perfect only when it is able in some way to provide an equivalent of the physical substance of expression.

I shall provide more examples to illustrate this in the next chapter, before approaching the problem of intersemiotic translation.

NOTES

1. Roman Jakobson, 'Linguistic aspects of translation', in Reuben A. Brower, ed., *On Translation* (Cambridge: Harvard U.P., 1959), pp. 232–9. See also Roman Jakobson, 'A few remarks on Peirce', *Modern Language Notes* xciii (1977), pp. 1026–36.
2. *Heraklit*, in *Gesamtausgabe* (Frankfurt: Klostermann, 1987).
3. Georg Gadamer, *Warheit und Methode* (Tübingen: Mohr, III, 1960).
4. George Steiner, *After Babel* (London: Oxford U.P., 1975), iv, 3.
5. *Quasi Come* (Milano: Bompiani, 1976).
6. Jacques Derrida wrote in *L'écriture et la différence* (Paris: Seuil, 1967, p. 312): 'A verbal body cannot be translated or transferred into another language. That's exactly what a translation drops. Let the body drop, this is the essential energy of translation.' But in the opening lecture of a symposium on translation held in Paris in December 1998 he said that a translation must be '*quantitatively equivalent* to the original [...] It is not the problem of counting the number of signs, of signifiers and signified, but rather of

counting the number of words [. . .] There is an ideal law, even though inaccessible: not to translate *word per word* or *word by word*, but to keep close as far as it is possible to the equivalence of a word *through* another word.'

7. New York: Basic Books, 1997, chapter 17.

8. *The Inferno of Dante*, tr. Robert Pinsky (New York: Farrar, Straus & Giroux, 1994).

9. *Dante's Inferno. Translations from Twenty Contemporary Poets* (New Jersey: Hopewell: Ecco Press, 1993).

10. *The Portable Dante* (New York: Penguin, 1995).

11. *The Divine Comedy – 1. Hell*, tr. Dorothy Sayers (Harmondsworth: Penguin, 1949–62).

12. *Poesie di T. S. Eliot*, tr. Luigi Berti (Parma: Guanda, 1949). T. S. Eliot, *Poesi*, tr. Roberto Sanesi (Milano: Bompiani, 1966).

13. T. S. Eliot, *Poèmes, 1910–1930, Texte anglais présenté et traduit par Pierre Leyris* (Paris: Seuil, 1947).

14. T. S. Eliot, *Poesie 1905/1920*, Italian tr. by Massimo Bagicalupo (Roma: Newton, 1996).

15. See for instance Itamar Even-Zohar, ed., 'Polysystems Studies', *Poetics Today* 11.1. (1990). See also Antoine Berman, *Pour une critique des traductions: John Donne* (Paris: Gallimard, 1995) and *La traduction et la lettre ou l'auberge lointain*, second edn (Paris: Seuil, 1999).

SEVEN

From substance to matter

Let me return to my personal experiences as a translator of Nerval's *Sylvie*, to further our discussion of the role of substance in texts aiming at an aesthetic effect.

Hidden verses

Before translating it I had read and reread *Sylvie* over a period of at least forty years. In spite of this it was only when I started my translation that I realised that, in certain scenes with a powerful dream-like quality, Nerval inserts 'lines of verse' – sometimes complete alexandrines, sometimes hemistichs, and sometimes hendecasyllables. The readers remain unaware of it (unless one reads the text out loud – as a translator must do if he or she wishes to discover the rhythm), but they are there and produce a sort of subliminal fascination.

For instance, in the second chapter (the dance on the lawn in front of the castle) there are at least sixteen such lines, including one hendecasyllable (*J'étais le seul garçon dans cette ronde*), alexandrines (like *Je ne pus m'empêcher / de lui presser la main*) and various hemistichs (like *La belle devait chanter*, or *Les longs anneaux roulés*). In the twelfth chapter, we find *Je jugeais que j'étais / perdu dans son esprit*.

I wanted to respect those rhythms that gave the text its dreamy charm, but I felt involved in a process of losses and compensations, since Italian did not always allow me to produce a line of verse in the same position in the syntactic string as Nerval's. Thus, when I lost the possibility of reproducing a verse where Nerval put it, I did my best to invent a verse immediately after, or before, to salvage the general effect, and to get an equivalent number of verses for every paragraph.

Let me quote only three examples, comparing the English translations of Halévy, Aldington and Sieburth. In the following quotations I shall put these lines in bold type to make them evident.

In chapter 3, when the Narrator (half asleep) evokes the vision of Adrienne we find:

> **Fantôme rose et blond / glissant sur l'herbe verte**, à demi baignée de blanches vapeurs.

One can miss every opportunity to save the rhythm, as Halévy did with his *A rosy and blond phantom **gliding over the green grass** that lay buried in white vapour.* One can miss the first verse and recuperate later, as Aldington did: *A rose and gold phantom **gliding over the green grass, / half bathed in white mists.*** Or one can give the translation an additional verse, as I did (with a double line of six syllables) and Sieburth also:

> Eco: **Fantasma rosa e biondo / lambente l'erba verde, / appena bagnata / di bianchi vapori.**

> Sieburth: **A phantom fair and rosy / gliding over the green grass / half bathed in white mist.**

They are not two cases of excessive generosity. Translators are frequently aware of having missed a chance or being on the verge of missing one, and thus try to recover their losses.

In chapter 3 we read:

> **Aimer une religieuse / sous la forme d'une actrice! . . . / et si c'était la même?** – Il y a de quoi devenir fou! c'est un entrainement fatal où l'inconnu vous attire **comme le feu follet** – fuyant sur les joncs d'une eau morte.

There are two alexandrines and two hemistichs. Halévy does not seem to have been sensitive to the rhythm, since he inserts lines, I think, at random, and not at strategic points. Probably his lines exemplify the hazards of a literal translation:

> To love a nun **in the form of an actress!** – and suppose **it was one and the same!** It was enough to drive one mad! **It is a fatal attraction** when the Unknown leads you on, **like the will-o'-the-wisp** that hovers over the rushes of a standing pool.

Aldington does not make any effort and his only hemistich is due to the fact – as for the other translators – that English probably has nothing better for *feu follet*:

> To love a nun in the shape of an actress . . . and suppose it was the same woman? It is maddening! It is fatal fascination where the unknown attracts you **like the will-o'-the-wisp** moving over the reeds of still water.

Sieburth, however, capitalises with two alexandrines and two hemistichs:

> **To be in love with a nun / in the guise of an actress!** . . . and what if they were one and the same! **It is enough to drive one mad** – the fatal lure of the unknown **drawing one ever onward / like a will o' the wisp / flitting over the rushes** of a stagnant pool.

I went further on, finding three complete alexandrines:

> *Amare una religiosa sotto le spoglie d'una attrice! . . . **e se fosse la stessa? / C'è da perderne il senno! / è un vortice fatale / a cui vi trae l'ignoto, / fuoco fatuo che fugge / su giunchi d'acqua morta . . .***

Perhaps I did too much, but I loved this 'singing' feel.

But Sieburth took his revenge in chapter 14, where we find these splendid closing lines:

Telles sont les chimères / qui charment et égarent / au matin de la vie. J'ai essayé de les fixer sans beaucoup d'ordre, *mais bien des cœurs me comprendront. Les illusions* **tombent l'une après l'autre, / comme les écorces d'un fruit,** *et le fruit, c'est l'experience.* **Sa saveur est amère:** *elle a pourtant quelque chose d'âcre qui fortifie.*

Nerval conceals in the text two alexandrines, a hendecasyllable and two more hemistichs. Translations follow, and Sieburth does his best to put the verses more or less where Nerval put them. This time his performance is better than mine. *Chapeau.*

Such are the charms that **fascinated and beguile us / in the morning of life. I have tried to depict them** without much order, but many hearts will understand me. **Illusions fall, like leaves,** one after another, and the kernel that is left when they are *stripped off is experience.* The taste is bitter, but it has an acid flavor that acts as a tonic. (Halévy)

Such are the delusions which charm and lead us astray **in the morning of life. / I have tried to set them down** in no particular order, but **there are many hearts / which will understand me.** Illusions fall one by one, **like the husks of a fruit, / and the fruit is experience.** Its taste is bitter, yet there is something sharp **about it which is tonic.** (Aldington)

Such are the chimeras / that beguile and misguide us / in the morning of life. / I have tried to set them down without much order, but many hearts will understand me. **Illusions fall away** one after another **like the husks of a fruit, / and that fruit is experience. It is bitter to the taste, but there is fortitude** to be found in gall. (Sieburth)

Tali son le chimere / che ammaliano e sconvolgono / all'alba della *vita. Ho cercato di fissarle senza badare all'ordine, ma molti cuori mi comprenderano. Le illusioni cadono l'una dopo l'altra,* **come scorze** *d'un frutto, / e il frutto è l'esperienza. Il suo sapore è amaro;* *e tuttavia esso ha qualcosa di aspro che tonifica.* (Eco)

Which translation is more faithful to Nerval's intention? I suggest the reader speak them aloud and decide which one 'sings' better – but reject those where the lines are too perceptible (I repeat: the verses should seduce the ear in a subliminal way without being immediately detectable).

Substance in poetic translations

A translation must preserve the textual rhythm. But that is not enough. As I have said in the previous chapters, many substances of expression are displayed on the expression plane and many of them are not specifically linguistic (such as metre and many phonosymbolic values). Metre is so independent from the structure of a given language that the same metric scheme can migrate from one language to another.

One of my favourite of Montale's poems is:

Addio, fischi nel buio, cenni, tosse
e sportelli abbassati: È l'ora. Forse
gli automi hanno ragione: Come appaiono
dai corridoi, murati! . . .

– Presti anche tu alla fioca
litania del tuo rapido quest'orrida
e fedele cadenza di carioca?

There are two translations of it, one in English by Katherine Jackson[1] and the other in French by Patrice Dyerval Angelini:[2]

Goodbyes, whistles in the dark, nods, coughing,
and train windows down. It's time. Perhaps
the robots are right. How they lean
from the corridors, walled in!

And do you too lend, to the dim
litany of your express train, this constant

fearful cadenza of a carioca? (Jackson)

Adieux, sifflets dans l'ombre, signes, toux
Et vitres fermées. C'est l'heure. Peut-être
Les automates ont-ils raison. Comme des couloirs
Il apparissent murés! . . .

Toi aussi, prêtes-tu à la sourde
Litanie de ton rapide cette affreuse
Et fidèle cadence de carioca? (Angelini)

A short comparison with the original tells us that in both translations the metre is not respected. Now metre is fundamental in this poem because (especially in the last tercet) the language reproduces both the rhythm of the train and the rhythm of the dance (*carioca*). I do not think that it is impossible to reproduce such a double rhythm in another language and I apologise for feeling obliged to quote a personal experience. I played many times with lipograms (a technique by which a given text is 'retold' once without using A, then without using E and so on – in fact one can make lipograms, as the old Greek poets did, for every letter of the alphabet). I also made *monovocalic* or one-vowel poems (in fact a monovocalic poem is a lipogram that avoids four vowels at the same time). Thus I tried to reproduce Montale's poem first as lipograms avoiding A, E, I, O and U, then as five monovocalic poems.[3]

My problem was certainly not to 'translate' the poem, but to save, with my pseudo-paraphrase, the *real thing*. And the real (poetic) thing was that in the poem there are five hendecasyllables, of which two are proparoxitone, and two seven-syllable verses; the first four verses are without rhyme and the last three with rhyme. In the first part of the poem there are *automi*, robots, and the last verse mentions a dance (*carioca*). My problem was to save all these features in every version, obviously by substituting the robots each time with a different mechanical entity (like a computer or a cyborg) and by finding for every lipogram a different dance. I reproduce here only the entire version of the A lipogram, for the other ones only the four last tercets:

Congedi, fischi, buio, cenni, tosse
e sportelli rinchiusi. È tempo. Forse
son nel giusto i robot. Come si vedono
nei corridoi, reclusi! . . .

— Odi pur tu il severo
sussulto del diretto con quest'orrido.
ossessivo ritorno di un bolero?

— Dona pur tu, su, prova
al litaniar di un rapido l'improvvido
ostinato ritmar di bossa nova . . .

— Do forse alla macumba
che danza questo treno la tremenda
ed ottusa cadenza di una rumba?

— Presti anche tu, chissà,
al litaniar dei rapidi quest'arida
cadenza di un demente cha-cha-cha?

— Non senti forse, a sera,
la litania del rapido nell'orrido
ancheggiare lascivo di habanera?

— Salta magra la gamba,
canta la fratta strada, pazza arranca,
assatanata d'asma l'atra samba?

— Del TEE presente
l'effervescenze fredde, le tremende
demenze meste d'ebete merenghe?

— Sì, ridi, ridi, insisti:
sibilin di sinistri ispidi brividi

misti ritmi scipiti, tristi twist.

– Colgo sol do-do-so . . .
Fosco locomotor, con moto roco
mormoro l'ostrogoto rock and roll.

– Ruhr, Turku . . . Timbuctù?
Uh, fu sul bus, sul currus d'un Vudù
un murmur (zum, zum, zum) d'un blu zulù.[4]

My question is the following: if it was possible to respect the real thing by using a crippled Italian, would it not have been possible to do the same with another language? I do not have an answer because I never tried to translate Montale into French or English but I suspect that it is possible. If the translators did not do that it was probably because they were more interested in the semantic side of their job (that is, in rendering the allegedly same linguistic meaning) than in the substantial aspects of the poem.

I think that playing with lipograms is a good way to understand what the 'real thing' of a poem is. Let us look at another of Montale's poems:

Spesso il male di vivere ho incontrato:
era il rivo strozzato che gorgoglia,
era l'incartocciarsi della foglia
riarsa, era il cavallo stramazzato.

Bene non seppi, fuori del prodigio
Che schiude la divina Indifferenza:
era la statua nella sonnolenza
del meriggio, e la nuvola, e il falco, alto levato.

This poem certainly has a semantic content, which can more easily be turned into a paraphrase than that of the previous poem. But the elements that show up in the poem – the rivulet, the leaf, the dead horse – become epiphanies of the 'evil of living' also because of the harshness of the adjectives and of the verbs the poet uses, such as *strozzato* or *gorgoglia*. Moreover, while the first eight verses are hendecasyllables, the last one has fourteen syllables, and this, with the aerial perspective of the cloud and of that hawk, as symbols of a non-terrestrial happiness, contributes to counteracting the feeling of evil: the last verse flies towards the skies, so to speak.

I tried five lipogrammatic variations of this poem[5] by respecting those essential characteristics. Once again I quote only the first variation (lipogram in A) and for the rest I cite only the last two lines:

> *Spesso il dolor di vivere l'ho intuito:*
> *fosse il rivo insistito che gorgogli,*
> *fosse il secco contorcersi di fogli*
> *combusti, od il corsiero indebolito.*
> *Bene non seppi, fuori del prodigio*
> *che schiude un cielo che si mostri inerte:*
> *forse l'idolo immoto su per l'erte*
> *del meriggio, od il corvo che voli, e l'infinito.*
>
> *dico la statua in una vuota stanza*
> *abbagliata, o la nuvola, o il falco, altro librato.*
>
> *era la statua nella sonnolenza*
> *dell'estate, o la nube, o un falco lato levato.*
>
> *Ed hai la statua nella stupescenza*
> *Di quest'alba, e la nube, se l'aquila si libra.*
>
> *era l'icona nella sonnolenza*
> *del meriggio, ed il cirro, ed il falco, alto levato.*

Let us now consider three translations.[6]

Often I have encountered the evil of living:
it was the strangled stream which gurgles,
it was the crumpling sound of the dried out
leaf, it was the horse sweaty and exhausted.

The good I knew not, other than the miracle
revealed by divine Indifference:
it was the statue in the slumber
of the afternoon, and the cloud, and the high flying falcon.
(Anonymous)

Often the pain of living have I met:
it was the choked stream that gurgles,
it was the curling up of the parched
leaf, it was the horse fallen off its feet.

Well-being I have not known, save the prodigy
that reveals divine Indifference:
it was the statue in the midday
somnolence, and the cloud, and the falcon high lifted. (Mazza)

Souvent j'ai rencontré le malheur de vivre:
c'était le ruisseau étranglé qui bouillonne,
c'était la feuille toute recoquillée
et acornie, c'était le cheval foudroyé.

Le bonheur je ne l'ai pas connu, hormis le prodige
qui dévoile la divine Indifférence:
c'était la statue dans la torpeur
méridienne, et le nuage
et le faucon qui plane haut dans le ciel. (Van Bever)

The three translators have respected Montale's *enjambements* and
did their best in choosing rough sounds; the two English versions give

a deeper breath to the last verse than the previous ones. Nevertheless none of the three has adopted a regular metre so as to be able to 'break' it in the last verse. Frankly I do not understand why.

A matter of matter

I would like to deal now with matters of matter or of continuum. As I said in chapter 1, a given language is born through the segmentation of a given expression continuum or matter. Taking the continuum into consideration can help us better to understand the differences between translation proper and the many kinds of so-called intersemiotic translation (or *transmutation*, in Jakobsonian terms), that I have decided to consider as cases of interpretation but not as cases of translation.

There are cases in which, in order to make the meaning of a word or of a sentence clear, we use an interpretant (in the Peircean sense) expressed in a different semiotic system. Think for instance what happens when I explain the sense of a verbal utterance by *ostension*, that is, when we use an object to 'translate' the meaning of a verbal expression, or the inverse, as when a child points his or her finger towards a car and I say that it is *a car*. In these cases, in order to explain the meaning or to help to isolate the referent of a term, we show an item belonging to the species named by that term and we teach not the proper name of that individual object but rather the common name of the species to which it belongs. If I ask *What is a baobab?* and someone shows me a baobab or the image of a baobab, I set up a cognitive scheme which allows me to recognise other baobabs in the future, even though partially different from the individual that has been shown to me.

In all the above cases, certainly, the new expression aims at interpreting a previous expression, but in different circumstances the same device could interpret different expressions. For instance, if I show someone a detergent box I can use it to better interpret a request like *Please buy me a box of the detergent so and so*, or in order to explain the meaning of the word *detergent* or even to provide an example of what I mean by *parallelepiped*.

If we use the term *to translate* in a metaphorical sense, many interpretations are forms of translation (and in the case of a silent language that reproduces the letters of the alphabet by given gestures it will be a form of transliteration). In passing from certain semiotic systems to others these forms of interpretation act as though they were interpretations by synonymy – with the same limits and strictures that hold for verbal synonymy.

But other cases would hardly be defined as translations, not even in a metaphorical sense. If one wants to explain the verbal expression *Beethoven's Fifth Symphony in C Minor*, one can undergo the effort of showing the 'real' musical object (by playing a disc or by taking the interlocutor to a concert hall). But usually one can sol-fa the beginning of that symphony (hoping that the musical memory of the interlocutor will do the rest). Likewise if somebody asks me what composition has just been broadcast on the radio, I can say it is Beethoven's Fifth Symphony in C Minor. A sufficient interpretation could also be to answer that this is one of Beethoven's symphonies.

Anyway, what characterises all those interpretations is the fact that the interpretant belongs to a different semiotic system from the *interpretandum*, and that their difference is due to the fact that their substance is produced by the segmentation of a different continuum or matter. If I recite *Hamlet* in Italian I change the form and the substance of the expression, but I remain within the boundaries of the same continuum or matter (sounds produced by a human throat). If on the contrary I represent Hamlet killing Polonius in a painting I have changed the expression matter.

Differences in continuum or matter are fundamental in a semiotic theory. Think for instance of the various debates on the presumed *omnipotence* or *effability* of verbal language. Lotman said that verbal language is *the primary modelling system* but it cannot translate everything into its own terms.

Hjelmslev[7] distinguished between *limited* and *unlimited* languages. For instance, the language of formal logic is limited in comparison to a natural language: given the most elementary logical formula ($p \supset q$) one can not only translate into English (*if P then Q*) but also variously interpret (*if smoke then fire, if fever then illness*), or even, counterfactually, *If Napoleon were a woman then he would have married Talleyrand*. On the contrary, given the sentence *If your son John has your own family name then it means that you have legally acknowledged him*, it is true that in a logical language it can be translated as p ⊃ q, but nobody could trace the original sentence from the formula.

It seems difficult to translate into words what is expressed by Beethoven's Fifth, as it is also impossible to 'translate' into music the whole *Critique of Pure Reason*. The phenomenon of ekphrasis permits one to describe an image by words, but no ekphrasis of *The Marriage of the Virgin* by Raphael can render either the perspective we see when looking at the painting, or the soft harmony of the colours.

Let us now consider the importance that a change in matter takes in cases of so-called intersemiotic translation, that one that Jakobson defined as *transmutation* and that is sometimes called *adaptation*.

Adaptations

The commonest cases concern the adaptation of a novel for a film, or occasionally for a theatrical piece, but there is also the adaptation of a fairy tale for a ballet, or for example, of a poem into a musical composition, of a musical composition into a painting or vice versa.

A translation proper can be made both in the presence of the original text and in its absence. Translations *in absentia* are more common but translations with the original text on the facing page are translations *in praesentia*. When one transmutes Debussy's *Prélude à l'après-midi d'un faune* into a ballet, we have music and choreographic movements together; on the other hand, when Debussy transmuted Mallarmé's *L'après-midi* from a poem into a musical composition, the orchestra was performing the musical score independently of the literary text.

Such transmutation can frequently serve to help appreciate the inspiring work better. We can speak of *understanding through manipulation*, and it is possible that after having listened to Debussy's composition one better appreciates Mallarmé's poetry. But it would be daring to say that Debussy has 'translated' Mallarmé.

Now, let us consider a ballet interpreting Debussy's *L'après-midi d'un faune*. If you cut off the sound, it is impossible to reconstruct the inspiring music from the visual choreography (one can at most guess that there is a story about some mythological beings). In the same vein, it is impossible to reconstruct the original poem from the music. Transmutation is not translation.

It has been said that certain paintings display particular linear tensions, like the direction of dynamic forces, and that those forces can be expressed by a musical composition. Correct, and perhaps the musical interpretation can help us better to understand the deep sense of the painting. But that painting probably exhibited colours or even recognisable images, and these features are obviously lost in the musical 'translation'. I admit that by synaesthesia it is possible to evoke colours through sounds, but no musical piece can allow one to recognise that the inspiring painting was a particular Miró or a particular Matisse.

If I read the French translation of an English poem I have many ways of figuring out what the original was or at least what it was about. If I listen to the musical composition without knowing the painting I have little chance of tracing the visual source.

In certain cases, we are prepared to accept a change of continuum, provided it is irrelevant for the purposes of interpretation. Let us suppose that in a school of architecture there is an exhibit featuring a scale model of Big Ben. Provided the proportions between the various elements of the model remain unchanged, the reduction in scale is not pertinent. Likewise, as long as the colour of the surfaces is the same, we can build the model in wood, clay or bronze. Modern museums have accustomed us to so-called artistic merchandising: they sell scale-model reproductions of famous works of art, be they the Venus de Milo or the head of Queen Nefertiti. However, if enjoyed for aesthetic reasons, such reproductions are obviously disappointing, because not only the real dimensions but also the tactile consistency of the original object are a part of the aesthetic enjoyment.

Adaptations say too much

When changing the continuum a phenomenon occurs that casts the idea of portraying a transmutation as a translation proper in doubt.

Jane Campion adapted Henry James's novel *Portrait of a Lady* into a movie.[8] The literary text says that Isabel *was better worth looking at than most works of art.* I do not think that James simply wanted to say that it was better to look at Isabel than to waste time in a museum: he certainly did want to say that Isabel had the same magic and charm as many art works or of many artistic representations of female beauty.

When reading James the reader remains free to imagine Isabel as like the *Primavera* of Botticelli, like Raphael's Fornarina, like a Pre-Raphaelite Beatrice, and even (*de gustibus non est disputandum ...*) like Picasso's *demoiselle d'Avignon.* Readers can use James's suggestion in order to picture a given visage according to their own ideal of womanly beauty.

It happens that in the movie Isabel is interpreted by Nicole Kidman. I personally like this actress, undoubtedly very beautiful, but I think that the movie would arouse different feelings if Isabel had the countenance of Greta Garbo or the Rubenesque features of Mae West. Thus the director has made the choice for me, and as a spectator I am less free than as a reader.

In the passage from one continuum to another we are forced to render explicit, and thus to emphasise, certain aspects of the content that a translation would have left indeterminate. I have already quoted Augusto Monterroso, who wrote the shortest tale in Western literature:

> *Cuando despertó, el dinosaurio todavía estaba allí.*

> (When he woke up, the dinosaur was still there.)

If one had to translate it into another language (as I have just done) it would be easy to retrieve the Spanish text from the English one.[9] Now, let us think of a movie director who wants to 'translate' this tale into a film. Apart from the fact that the movie would have to show the protagonist as male or female, the director cannot simply show a sleeping person who, when he/she awakes, sees a dinosaur. He would thus lose the sense of that *todavia*. At this point the director would realise that this short tale suggests at least two different stories: (i) a person is awake, close to a dinosaur; in order to avoid such a disturbing experience he/she falls alseep, and on waking sees that the monster is still there; (ii) a person is awake, without dinosaurs around, he/she falls asleep, dreams of a dinosaur, and on waking realises that the dinosaur from his/her dreams is still there. It goes without saying that the second reading is, in both a surrealistic and Kafkaesque mode, wittier than the first one.

One is obliged to choose only one of these two interpretations and, even though unable to produce a version as essential as the original, one could produce something that could be summarised either as (a) as he/she woke up, the dinosaur that he/she tried to ignore was still there, or (b) as he/she woke up, the dinosaur that he/she dreamt of was still there.

Let us suppose that a director chooses the second interpretation. Considering that a film must last at least a few seconds, there are only four possibilities: (i) one starts by imagining that a person dreams of a dinosaur, wakes up and sees that the dinosaur is still there – and then one could develop a story with a series of events, perhaps very surreal, which the verbal tale does not make explicit but which could explain what really happened; (ii) one represents a series of everyday events and by complicating them ends with the episode of the dream and of the waking up; (iii) one tells various aspects of the life of the main character by reiterating obsessively the experience both of the dream and of the dinosaur; (iv) one decides to make an avant-garde movie by repeating for three hours the same scene (dream and awakening), in the same vein in which Andy Warhol showed the same image of the Empire State Building for several hours.

Now let us ask the spectators of our four possible movies to summarise them. It seems to me verisimilar that the spectators of (i) and (ii) will be able to identify one aspect of that oneiric experience as more pertinent than others, but I do not know which one because I have not seen the movie. Spectators of version (iii) could say that the movie tells about a recurrent oneiric situation concerning a dinosaur, which was first a dream-like figure and then a real one. Even though the second ones would have better realised the spirit of Monterroso's story, they would be unable to rephrase it literally as it was originally. Spectators of version (iv), if very fussy, would say that:

When he woke up, the dinosaur was still there.
When he woke up, the dinosaur was still there.
When he woke up, the dinosaur was still there.
When he woke up, the dinosaur was still there.
(and so on *ad infinitum*),

which seems more like an avant-garde poem than a report on a new movie.

In chapter 10 of *The Betrothed*, after having spoken at length about Egidio's seduction of the Nun of Monza, Manzoni, in a passage of great decency, in a brief sentence, gives the reader to understand that the Nun surrendered to her seducer: *La sventurata rispose.* An English version reads *The poor wretch answered* and a French one *L'infortunée répondit.*[10]

Later, the novel tells us that the Nun slid into a criminal life. But Manzoni does not tell us what happened between her answer and the moment she became guilty of many crimes. The gravity of her fall is only suggested by that lapidary sentence that implies both a moral judgement and compassion. It is the reader who must interpret that reticence. Manzoni was very prudish and never mentioned a sexual scene.

Manzoni's novel has been the subject of various versions for both television and cinema. Directors had to *show* us the answer of the Nun – not necessarily as sexual intercourse but at least as a moment – thus showing a face, a gesture, a smile, a gleam in the eye, a tremor. They were obliged to 'say' if she was happy, excited, or tortured by lacerating qualms of conscience. They had to make us see in some way the intensity of that answer, which the written text left indeterminate. In transmuting the verbal text into another continuum, a moviemaker is obliged to compel the spectators to accept a given visual interpretation of a verbal reticence.

In the shift from continuum to continuum the interpretation is mediated by somebody who acts as a gatekeeper reducing freedom of the addressee.

Adaptations say too little

But adaptations do not only run the risk of saying too much. Sometimes the opposite occurs.

The Mozarabic illuminators who made those marvellous manuscripts called the *Beati*, illustrating the *Commentary to the Book of Revelation* by Beatus de Liébana, were supposed to illustrate the various pages of St John's Book. Apparently they had great difficulty in rendering this passage from chapter 4:

> A throne was set in heaven, and one sat on the throne. And he that sat was to look upon like a jasper and a sardine stone: and there was a rainbow round about the throne, in sight like unto an emerald. And round about the throne were four and twenty seats; and upon the seats I saw four and twenty elders sitting, clothed in white raiment; and they had on their heads crowns of gold. And out of the throne proceeded lightnings and thunderings and voices: and there were seven lamps of fire burning before the throne, which are the Seven Spirits of God. And before the throne there was a sea of glass like unto crystal; and in the midst of the throne, and round about the throne, were four beasts full of eyes before and behind.

A prime instance of hypotyposis, indeed. Now, hypotyposis uses words in order to encourage the addressee to build up a visual representation. But this demands the cooperation of the reader. The big difficulty experienced by Mozarabic artists was to represent the four strange creatures standing *in the midst of the throne, and round about the throne* – or, as the Latin Vulgata, the only version they knew, said, *super thronum et circa thronum*. How can these four creatures sit *on* or *upon and around* the throne at the same time?

Moreover, St John's vision came from the vision of Ezekiel, and the illuminators knew that text. It says (according to the King James version, chapter 1, vv. 4–26):

And I looked, and, behold, a whirlwind came out of the north, a great cloud, and a fire infolding itself, and a brightness was about it, and out of the midst thereof as the colour of amber, out of the midst of the fire. Also out of the midst thereof came the likeness of four living creatures. And this was their appearance; they had the likeness of a man. And every one had four faces, and every one had four wings. And their feet were straight feet; and the sole of their feet was like the sole of a calf's foot: and they sparkled like the colour of burnished brass. And they had the hands of a man under their wings on their four sides; and they four had their faces and their wings. Their wings were joined one to another; they turned not when they went; they went every one straight forward . . .

Now as I beheld the living creatures, behold one wheel upon the earth by the living creatures, with his four faces. The appearance of the wheels and their work was like unto the colour of a beryl: and they four had one likeness: and their appearance and their work was as it were a wheel in the middle of a wheel. When they went, they went upon their four sides: and they turned not when they went . . . And when the living creatures went, the wheels went by them: and when the living creatures were lifted up from the earth, the wheels were lifted up . . . And above the firmament that was over their heads was the likeness of a throne, as the appearance of a sapphire stone . . .

An examination of the solutions given by the various *Beati* shows us that this is an impossible situation, giving rise to representations which do not 'translate' the text satisfactorily. The images seem unable to decide where the hell these four damned beasts were, and in which position, or what the wheels looked like.

This occurred because the illuminators, brought up in the Greek Christian tradition, thought that the prophet 'saw' something similar to statues and paintings. But both John the Apostle and Ezekiel came from the Jewish tradition, which was not visually, but aurally oriented and, what's more, their imaginations were those of seers. Therefore, John was not describing something similar to a statue or to a painting, but rather a dream – and dreams are more similar to movies than to miniatures. In a film-like vision, the creatures can wheel and appear simultaneously on, in front of, and around the throne. In a miniature they must remain in one place.

In this instance the Mozarabic miniaturists could not cooperate with the text, and somehow, in their hands – under their pen or brush – and in their minds, hypotyposis failed.

For mysterious reasons the illuminator of the *Apocalypse of Saint Sever* represents a happy exception to the rule. He puts the beasts at different distances from the throne and one of them seems on the verge of passing through it. Maybe that artist had a vague intuition of what was really happening in both the visions and he did his best to express a sort of spiral-like translation. He did his best, but he could not completely achieve what he probably intended to do: the change in the expression continuum froze his intuition. As Sol Worth once said, 'Pictures can't say ain't', but I would add that pictures frequently cannot say 'I am moving this or that way'. Probably a futurist painter like Boccioni could have succeeded in doing so, but Mozarabic illuminators couldn't. There are things one can do with a movie but not with a painting. The verbal text suggested more than its visual transmutation and the change of continuum humiliated the vision.

Who is speaking in Pinocchio?

Pinocchio by Carlo Collodi begins with:

C'era una volta . . .
– Un re! – diranno subito i miei piccoli lettori.

– No ragazzi, avete sbagliato. C'era una volta un pezzo di lengo.

An early English translation by M. A Murray (1883) reads:

There was once upon a time . . .
'A king!' my little readers will instantly exclaim.
No, children, you are wrong. There was once upon a time a piece of wood.

It is correct. But let's see what happens with a French translation:[11]

– Il était une fois . . .
– UN ROI, direz-vous?
– Pas du tout, mes chers petits lecteurs. Il était une fois . . . UN MORCEAU DE BOIS!

In this translation *Il était une fois* (Once upon a time) is introduced by a dash as if a *dramatis persona,* that is, one of the characters of the novel, were speaking. Thus the reader is led to believe that the second line represents a conversational turn, and that some kids are reacting to the first speaker. At this point, even the *direz-vous* seems to be pronounced by the kids. On the contrary (and that is why Collodi did not open the first line with a dash or with inverted commas), the one who is speaking at the beginning is the Narrator (standing outside the story and summoning his ideal little readers). Thus even the second line does not represent a conversation taking place between characters, but rather a sort of metafictional device, by which the Voice of the Narrator evokes his ideal readers, attributing to them a mistake (an understandable one, indeed, since usually kids are accustomed to fairy tales beginning with kings or princesses) and immediately after disenchanting them, saying that his own is a different and unheard-of tale. Then, after that metafictional warning, the story starts.

The strategy of Collodi is very subtle, because it is doubtful whether he really conceived of his story as a simple tale for kids, and there are a considerable number of 'adult' interpretations of *Pinocchio* as a very complex allegory. However, that French translation, by a simple misuse of dashes, eliminates any possible more sophisticated reading. In a way we can say that Murray's version overinterprets Collodi's intention, by eliminating the last dash, but reinforces the metanarrative device.

Now let us come to the filmic adaptation of *Pinocchio* by Walt Disney. Collodi's devotees can say that Disney changed the story to some extent, that Cricket is not longer a severe pedagogue but rather a nice vaudeville character and so on, but these are not relevant objections. The real problem is that Disney did not dare to put the voice of the Narrator at the beginning, and if he had done so he would have had problems in evoking the voice of the kids. So they gave the floor directly to Jiminy Cricket, who is at the same time the narrator of the story and one of its characters. Thus there is no more metafictional strategy and a tale that was narrated in the third person by an uncommitted Voice becomes a tale narrated in the first person by one of the *dramatis personae*. *Pinocchio* as a movie has lost any wink to its possible adult spectators.

Deathblow in Venice

One of the most blatant cinematic misinterpretations of a book is the movie by Luchino Visconti, *Death in Venice*, drawn from Thomas Mann's novella. I myself have argued that when Visconti transformed *The Leopard* of Tomasi di Lampedusa into a movie, he successfully helped his spectators to understand the deep sense of the novel.

Not so with *Death in Venice*. Mann's main character, Gustav Aschenbach, is a fifty-year-old writer (therefore, in those times, a very old man); he comes from a high bourgeois family of austere state servants; he is a historian and an art critic (one of his essays was entitled 'Spirit and Art'); and he shares with many German intellectuals of his generation a neoclassical love for pure, Platonic, ideal beauty.

Having a classical temperament, he is immediately faced with the romantic and decadent nature of Venice. When first setting eyes on the adolescent Tadzio, who will later become the object of his love and lust, he admires him as something similar to Greek statues of the golden period, as a pure perfection of form. Aschenbach's remarks are always referring to his classical culture to the extent that many visions of the sea remind him of figures in Hellenic mythology. The tragedy of Aschenbach, when he realises that he physically desires Tadzio, consists in discovering that his purely Platonic sense of beauty was step by step becoming a carnal passion. In the background, there is an implicit criticism of the aesthetic ideals of neoclassical art historians *à la* Winckelmann, whose sincere and spiritualised artistic taste was in fact the sublimation of homosexual drives.

That's the tragedy of Aschenbach: he cannot accept the revelation that his aesthetic ideals were disguising a more terrestrial excitement – and at the same time he cannot resist his carnal tumult. *Death in Venice* tells the story of a victory of Dionysos against Apollo.

What happens with the movie? Visconti probably found that it was difficult to represent the aesthetic ideals of the old man visually; probably he was misled by that name, Gustav, which evoked Gustav Mahler. Aschenbach therefore became a musician. It is true that in a few flashbacks we follow a dialogue between him (supporting a classical idea of art and beauty as order and detachment from passion) and his friend (who extols a more Romantic idea of the artistic genius), but these are mere words. Spectators are fascinated by the sound, and the sound is provided by the music of Mahler, which becomes the 'real' manifestation of the inner feelings of the protagonist. Aschenbach speaks as if he were Bach, but *we hear* Mahler.

Mann's Aschenbach is a mature and old-fashioned gentleman – and this makes his slow transformation more tragic and unacceptable for him – while Visconti's Aschenbach looks younger, fragile, psychologically tortured, already ill, ready to identify himself with a dilapidated Venice morbid in its refined social rites. Moreover,

Mann's Aschenbach comes from a bourgeois family and received his 'von' very late, as an award for merit, while Visconti's Aschenbach appears immediately as a Gustav *von* Aschenbach, and as such is already marked by the symptoms of a decadent nobility and looks more similar to Huysmans' Des Esseintes than to a severe scholar. He is already as voluptuous and condemned to death as Venice.

His attraction for Tadzio is immediate, while in Mann's story it takes time for Aschenbach to shift from his Hellenistic fantasies to the acceptance of the real passion that stirs him. Besides, in the novel Tadzio is fourteen years old and there is no shadow of malice in the few glances and in the only smile he addresses to his mature admirer. In the movie Tadzio is a little older and every time he looks at Aschenbach his gaze is far more ambiguous.

Where then in the film is the opposition between two ethical and artistic ideals? Why should Visconti's Aschenbach be so troubled by a not-so-unexpected temptation, why should he feel it as radically and tragically perverse – despite the fact that Visconti reminds us at times of the existence of a gracious wife and of a daughter? Does Aschenbach suffer because he feels unfaithful to his wife or rather because he realises that his whole spiritual world and his algid cult of beauty are turning upside-down? Mann's Aschenbach cannot stand the discovery that his aesthetic ideals were simply the disguise of a sexual turmoil.

The plot remains more or less the same: there is still Venice, an artist, a boy, many minor characters, and there is the obsessive presence of the pestilence slowly sneaking up on the city, a metaphor for the growing moral disease of the artist. But the decision to change the occupation and the features of Aschenbach has produced a radical change to the whole story.

Let us say that Visconti *wanted* to provide a deliberately different interpretation of Mann's novel. Frequently transmutations represent a *critical standpoint*. Naturally, even a translation proper implies, with an interpretation, a critical standpoint. But in translation the critical attitude of the translator is in fact implicit (as were the translations of *la sventurata rispose*, which show how the translators correctly interpreted the intention of the text and attempted to convey that intention to their readers). Translators are duty-bound not to say more than the original text, while in transmutation the critical intention of the 'adapter' becomes preponderant, and represents the very essence of the whole process. Adaptations frequently produce not only variations in expression but also a substantial change in content.

Adaptation, use and interpretation

Spaziante[12] suggests that for many cases of adaptation one could speak (following the distinction I posited in *The Role of the Reader* and *The Limits of Interpretation*), of *use* rather than *interpretation* of a text. One can *use* a text in many ways (one can even use the pages of a book to light a fire), and among them there are very respectable practices: one can use a poem or a novel as opportunities for daydreaming, to muse about personal experiences and memories, which do not come from the original text. In my previous writings I defined as mere use certain deconstructive drifts that follow the principle that *il n'y a pas de vrai sense d'un texte*, but I was not considering the use of a text as a censurable habit.

Anybody, on occasion, can listen to a Chopin waltz and (instead of following the musical discourse attentively) indulge in remembering a time when it was heard next to a beloved – and many people will play a song again when wanting to regain a lost moment in time (as Rick Blaine does in his Café Americain in *Casablanca*).

Among the infinite ways to use a text there is also the custom of starting from a stimulus text in order to get ideas for creating one's own text. One can write a sequel to *Gone with the Wind*, rewrite *Sylvie* from Sylvie's point of view, emulate a great author – as Sophocles did when writing his own *Oedipus Rex* after Aeschylus's *Oedipus*. Many adaptations are therefore excellent examples of creative use of a previous text. But insofar as they are freely creative, they are not translations, since a translator has always to tame, in some way, his or her 'creative' impetus.

Demoiselle d'Avignon

To come back to more terrestrial and profane experiences, I remember a pleasant party where at one stage we played an old game known in Italian as *Le belle statuine*, the beautiful statuettes. A given group had to represent visually, each using their own body, a work of art (a novel, a movie, a painting and so on). Three girls performed a very swift event, disarticulating their limbs, twisting their bodies and grimacing – and they looked cute and provocative at the same time.

Everybody (or at least the smartest among the onlookers) immediately recognised Picasso's *Les demoiselles d'Avignon*. Nevertheless I do not think that somebody who had never seen that painting would have been able to reconstruct or even figure out the original work from that performance. That representation emphasised the non-realistic and primitive force of the original work, perhaps overstressed a visual rhythm, but was unable to suggest the colours, the contour of the figures, the strokes of the brush – moreover, it was also misleading from the point of view of the expressed content, since the *demoiselles* of Picasso are five and not three.

These *demoiselles* were a witty instance of transmutation, not a serious example of translation. I admit that it was a nice case of interpretation. But as I have tried to demonstrate, the universe of interpretations is massively larger and more multifarious than the territory of transmutation.

NOTES

1. *I Mottetti by Eugenio Montale*, tr. Katherine Jackson (I found it at world.std.com/~jpwilson/kjbio.html).
2. *Poèmes choisis*, tr. Patrice Dyerval Angelini (Paris: Gallimard, 1991).
3. 'Undici danze per Montale', in *Il Secondo Diario Minimo* (Milano: Bompiani, 1992), pp. 278–81.
4. Obviously I knew that a blue is not a dance, but try to find another dance by using only the U . . .
5. In *Vocali* (Napoli: Guida, 1991).

6. I found the first English one on an Internet site that, as usual, does not provide any bibliographical reference (www.geocities.com/Paris/LeftBank/5739/eng-living.html). The last two are respectively from *The Bones of Cuttlefish*, tr. Antonino Mazza (Oakville: Mosaic Press, 1983) and *Montale traduit par Pierre Van Bever* (Collection bilingue de poésie de l'Institut Culturel Italien de Paris, 1968).

7. 'The Basic Structure of Language', 1947. In *Essais linguistiques II*, Travaux du Cercle Linguistique de Copenhague (1973), pp. 119–56.

8. Cf. Gian Paolo Caprettini, 'Itinerari della mente cinematografica', in Nicola Dusi and Siri Nergaard, eds., *Sulla traduzione intersemiotica*, special issue of *VS* lxxxv–lxxxvii (2000), pp. 133–42.

9. However, in English one is obliged to give the character a gender, while the Spanish text remained uncommitted.

10. *The Betrothed*, tr. Bruce Penman (Harmondsworth: Penguin, 1972); *Les fiancés*, tr. Yves Braca (Paris: Gallimard, 1995).

11. *Les aventures de Pinocchio*, tr. Nicolas Cazelles (Arles: Actes Sud, 1995).

12. Lucio Spaziante, 'L'ora della ricreazione', in Dusi and Nergaard, eds., pp. 235–50.

EIGHT

A conclusion on perfect language and colours

In the preceding seven chapters I have repeatedly spoken of negotiation. Translators must negotiate with the ghost of a distant author, with the disturbing presence of foreign text, with the phantom of the reader they are translating for. Translation is a negotiation to such an extent that translators must also negotiate with publishers, because a translation may be more or less domesticated or foreignised according to the context in which the book is published, or the age of its expected readers.

Can one avoid negotiating and rely on a sort of golden rule which acts as a parameter in order to accept or reject a translation as the most faithful one? Yes. We can refuse negotiation as a vicious habit if we can refer to a Perfect Language.

Perfect languages

What was the exact nature of the gift of tongues received by the apostles? Reading St Paul (Corinthians 1:12–13) it seems that the gift was that of *glossolalia* – that is, the ability to express oneself in an ecstatic language that everybody can understand as if it were his own native speech. Reading the Acts of the Apostles chapter 2, however, we discover that at Pentecost a loud roar was heard from the skies, and that upon each of the apostles a tongue of flame descended, and they started to speak in *other* languages. In this case, the gift was not *glossolalia* but *xenoglossia*, that is, polyglottism – or, failing that, at least a sort of mystic service of simultaneous translation. The question of which interpretation to accept is not really a joking matter: there is a major difference between the two accounts. In the first hypothesis, the apostles would have been restored to the conditions before Babel, when all mankind spoke but a single holy dialect. In the second hypothesis, the apostles were granted the gift of momentarily reversing the defeat of Babel, and of no longer finding in the multiplicity of tongues a wound that must, at whatever cost, be healed, but rather the possibility of a new alliance and of a new concord.

Between the tenth and the eleventh centuries, there was an Arab writer, Ibn Hazm, who told the myth of Babel in a different way. In the beginning there existed a single language given by God, a language thanks to which Adam was able to understand the quiddity of things. It was a language that provided a name for every thing, be it substance or accident. But if in a language an abundance of homonyms can produce equivocation – since a single word can be variously interpreted as referring to different things and concepts according to the circumstance of utterance – an abundance of synonyms would not jeopardise the perfection of a language. It is possible to name the same thing in different ways, provided we do so in an adequate way.

Thus for Ibn Hazm the original language was so rich in synonyms that it *included every possible language.* The *confusio* did not depend on the invention of new languages, but on the fragmentation of a unique tongue that existed *ab initio* and in which all the others were already contained. It is for this reason that all men are still able to understand the revelation of the Koran, in whatever language it is expressed. God made the Koranic verses in Arabic so that they might be understood by His chosen people, not because the Arabic language enjoyed any particular privilege. In any language men may discover the spirit, the breath, the perfume, and the traces of the original multilingualism.

The intuition that the problem of translation itself presupposed a perfect language is already present in Walther Benjamin: since it is impossible to reproduce all the linguistic meanings of the source language in a target language, one is forced to place one's faith on the convergence of all languages. In each language taken as a whole, there is a self-identical thing that is meant, a thing that, nevertheless, is accessible to none of these languages taken individually, but only to that totality of all their intentions taken as reciprocal and complementary – a totality that we call Pure Language (*reine Sprache*[1]). This *reine Sprache* is not a real language. If we think of the mystic and Kabbalistic sources that were the inspiration for Benjamin's thinking, we begin to sense the impending ghost of sacred languages, of something more akin to the secret genius of Pentecostal languages than to the ideal of the *a priori* languages. As Derrida said, 'Even the desire for translation is unthinkable without the *correspondence* with the thought of God.'[2]

In many of the most notable projects for mechanical translation there exists a notion of a parameter language, which shares many of the characteristics of a perfect language. There must exist, it is argued, a *tertium comparationis*, which might allow us to shift from an expression in language Alpha to an expression in language Beta by deciding that both are equivalent to an expression of a mental language Gamma. If such a *tertium comparationis* really existed, it would be a perfect language; if it did not exist, it would remain a mere postulate on which every translation ought to depend.

The criterion of textual relevance becomes more important when we are dealing not with the translation of isolated words but rather with the translation of sentences. If for isolated words there is a dictionary, sentences designate states of affairs which are not registered by any dictionary.

According to certain philosophers of language two sentences uttered in two different languages are equivalent if they express the same proposition. What is the criterion for stating that two sentences in two different languages convey the same proposition? In order to realise that the sentences *Io ti amo, Je t'aime, I love you, Ich liebe dich, Te amo* express the same proposition, we ought to be able to express that constant proposition in a sort of mental language common to every culture and independent of the single tongues. Such a mental language would meet the requirements of that Perfect or Adamic or Universal Language that so many have dreamt of over the centuries – with which I have dealt in *The Search for a Perfect Language*, born from a series of lectures I gave in Oxford in 1991.[3]

A mental language does not necessarily have to be of divine origin, but it should be rooted in the universal workings of the human mind. Moreover, its propositions should be expressible in a formalised language. Such a mental language will then represent a *tertium comparationis* that allows the passage of an expression from language Alpha to an expression in language Beta by ensuring that both are equivalent to an expression in mental language Gamma.

But such a solution cannot avoid the classical objection of the Third Man. If, in order to translate a sentence A, expressed in a language Alpha, into a sentence B, expressed in a language Beta (and to say that B is a correct translation of A, and is similar in meaning to A) one must pass through the mental language Gamma, then one is obliged first of all to decide in which way A and B are similar in meaning to a sentence X in Gamma. But, to decide this, one requires a new language Delta, and so on *ad infinitum*.

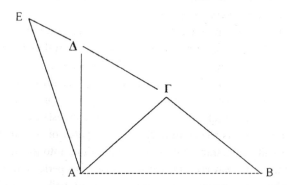

I am not saying that it is impossible to isolate, for two different sentences A and B in two different languages, a proposition X that expresses the same content as A and B. Such a proposition can be found (and made perceptible as a sentence in any third language, be it formalised or not) and it would be a reasonable interpretation of both A and B. What I am trying to say is that such a proposition will not be the parameter for establishing a similarity in meaning between A and B, as if such a similarity existed in a sort of Platonic world before the process of translation was started. The recognised similarity will rather be the final result of a successful act of translation.

The only alternative is to discover a natural language which is so 'perfect' (so flexible and powerful) as to serve as a *tertium comparationis*. In 1603, the Jesuit Ludovico Bertonio published his *Arte de lengua Aymara* (which he supplemented in 1612 with a *Vocabulario de la lengua Aymara*). Aymara is a language (still partially spoken by Indians living between Bolivia and Peru), and Bertonio discovered that it displayed an immense flexibility and capability to accommodate neologisms, and was particularly adapted to the expression of abstract concepts, so much so as to raise a suspicion that it was an artificial invention. In 1860 Emeterio Villamil de Rada (in his *La lengua de Adan*) described it as the language of Adam, the expression of 'an idea anterior to the formation of language', founded upon 'necessary and immutable ideas' and, therefore, a philosophical language if ever there were one.

Recent studies have established that unlike Western thought, based on a two-valued logic (either True or False), Aymara thought is based on a three-valued logic, and is, therefore, capable of expressing modal subtleties which other languages can only capture through complex circumlocutions. Thus, to finish, there have been proposals to use Aymara to resolve all problems of computer translation. Unfortunately, owing to its algorithmic nature, the syntax of Aymara would greatly facilitate the translation of any other idiom into its own terms, but not the other way around. Thus, because of its perfection, Aymara can render every thought expressed in other mutually untranslatable languages, but the price of this is that once the perfect language has resolved these thoughts into its own terms, they cannot be translated back into our natural native idioms.[4]

One way out of this dilemma is to assume, as certain authors have recently done, that translation is a matter to be resolved entirely within the destination (or target) language, according to the context. This means that it is within the framework of the target language that all the semantic and syntactic problems posed by the source-text must be resolved. This is a solution that takes us outside the problem of perfect languages, or of a *tertium comparationis*, for it implies that we need to understand expressions formed according to the genius of the source language and to invent a 'satisfying' paraphrase according to the genius of the target language. Yet how are we to establish what the criteria of 'satisfaction' should be?

These were theoretical difficulties that Humboldt had already foreseen. If no word in a language exactly corresponds to a word in another one, translation would be impossible. At most, translation is an activity, in no way regulated, through which we are able to understand what our own language was unable to say.

Yet if translation implied no more than this it would be subject to a curious contradiction: the possibility of a relation between two languages, Alpha and Beta, only occurs when Alpha is closed in a full realisation of itself, assuming that it has understood Beta, of which nothing can be any longer said, for all that Beta had to say is by now said by Alpha.

Comparison

It has been repeatedly said that, in order to interpret our actual world (or the possible ones of which many of the texts we translate speak) we are moving within the framework of a semiotic system that society, history, education have organised for us. It has been said that we are defined by our language, and in this sense Barthes once said that language is radically fascist. If this is true, then any translation of a text coming from another language and another culture would be impossible. To repeat Quine, one cannot express in a jungle language a sentence such as *neutrinos lack mass*.

However the experiences we have analysed up to now have shown us that, to a certain extent, it is possible to translate. If different linguistic systems still look mutually *incommensurable*, they remain mutually *comparable*. Linguists and semioticians have been black-mailed for years by the idea that Eskimos have many different names to identify what we call *snow*, according to its physical state, but eventually it has become evident that they are not at all prisoners of their own language and understand perfectly well that when we say *snow* we speak of something similar to the different things they name individually. I pointed out in my first essay that Italians do not make any lexical distinction between *grandson* and *nephew*, and call both *nipote* (which at the beginning of an interaction may produce some misunderstanding), but they clearly have in their minds the difference between the son of their son or daughter, and the son of their brother or sister. A French person uses the same word, *glace*, to refer to both ice and ice-cream, but French people (even though they eat frogs and drive on the wrong side) do not put ice-cream cubes in their Scotch, nor even in their Pernod.

Thus, rather than a powerful metalanguage, we might elaborate a comparative tool, not itself a language, which might (if only approximately) be expressed in any language, and which might, furthermore, allow us to compare any two linguistic structures that seemed, in themselves, incommensurable. This instrument or procedure would be able to function in the same way and for the same reason that any natural language is able to translate its own terms into others by an *interpretative principle*: according to Peirce, any natural language can serve as a metalanguage for itself.

See for instance a table created by Nida[5] that displays the semantic differences in a number of verbs of motion.

	RUN	WALK	HOP	SKIP	JUMP	DANCE	CRAWL
1. one or another limb always in contact vs no limb at times in contact	−	+	−	−	−	±	+
2. order of contact	1-2-1-2	1-2-1-2	1-1-1 or 2-2-2	1-1-2-2	not relevant	variable but rhythmic	1-3-2-4
3. number of limbs	2	2	1	2	2	2	4

We can regard this table as an example of an attempt to illustrate, in English – as well as by other semiotic means – what a certain class of English terms mean. Naturally, the interpretative principle demands that the English speaker also interpret the meaning of *limb*, as indeed any other term appearing in the interpretation of the verbal expression. The eighteenth-century philosopher and linguist Degérando observed that in order to analyse even an apparently primitive term such as *to walk* there will be an infinite regression. It has been said that it is easier to define the word *infarct* than the verb *to be*. However, Nida's table can be used by anybody who has assumed that terms such as *limbs* or *contact* are primitives.

Translation proceeds according to the same principle, and once again we are faced with negotiation processes. If one wished, for example, to translate Nida's table from English into Italian, we would probably start by substituting for the English verbs, Italian terms that are practically synonymous: *correre* for *to run*, *camminare* for *to walk*, *danzare* for *to dance*, and *strisciare* for *to crawl*. As soon as we got the verb *to hop*, we would have to pause; there is no direct synonym in Italian for an activity that the Italian–English dictionary might define as 'jumping on one leg only'. Nor is there an adequate Italian synonym for the verb *to skip*: Italian has various terms, such as *saltellare*, *ballonzolare*, and *salterellare*; these can approximately render *to skip*, but they can also translate as *to frisk*, *to hop*, or *to trip*, and thus do not uniquely specify the sort of alternate hop-shuffle-step movement specified by the English *to skip*.

Even though Italian lacks a term which adequately conveys the meaning of *to skip*, the rest of the terms in the table – *limb*, *order of contact*, *number of limbs* – are all definable, if not necessarily by Italian synonyms, at least by means of references to contexts and circumstances. Even in English, we have to conjecture that, in this table, the term *contact* must be understood as 'contact with the surface the movement takes place upon' rather than 'contact with another limb'. To either define or translate, we thus do not need a fully fledged metalanguage at our disposition. We assume that all languages have some notion that corresponds to the term *limb*, because all humans have a similar anatomy. Furthermore, all cultures probably have ways of distinguishing hands from arms, palms from fingers, and, on fingers, the first joint from the second, and the second from the third; and this assumption would be no less true even in a culture such as Father Mersenne imagined, in which every individual pore, every convolute of a thumbprint had its own individual name. Thus, by starting from terms whose meanings are known and working to interpret by various means (perhaps even with gestures) terms whose meanings are not known, proceeding by successive adjustments, an English-speaker would be able to convey to an Italian-speaker what the phrase *John hops* is all about.

A parenthesis on translation and ontology

It is possible to compare the structure of two languages Alpha and Beta by referring two different terms A and B to the same human behaviour (i.e. jumping or crawling) or to a common parental relationship. Despite the fact that the French *bois* covers a semantic space different from the one covered by the Italian *bosco*, we are able to detect whether a French speaker is speaking of a collection of trees or of the material used to make a chair – and so on. Such remarks suggest two possible ontological solutions: (i) there are universal ways of segmenting the continuum of human experience even though our languages sometimes blur them; (ii) in the continuum of our experience there is (as I suggested in *Kant and the Platypus*) a 'hard core of Being', not something tangible and solid, as if it were a 'kernel' that, by biting into it, we might one day reveal, but rather some *lines of resistance* – by virtue of which, for instance, we can speak in every language of crawling, hopping or jumping human beings but not, and in no case, of flying humans.

If so, and irrespective of the solution, we should say that, even though no perfect language can univocally express these universal phenomena, it would be with them that languages should be confronted.

It is curious to remark that, while so many philosophical discussions have cast doubt on the very possibility of translation, since each language represents an incommensurable structure, it is precisely the empirical evidence of translation that challenges the philosophical assertions about the dependence of world views on language. Thus translation re-proposes to philosophy its everlasting question, namely, whether there is a way in which *things go*, independently of the way our languages make them go.

I do not feel compelled to deal now with such a tremendous question because I did it in *Kant and the Platypus*. But as far as the more modest problem of translation is concerned, we can simply and prudently remark that a comparison between two linguistic systems allows us to solve many conundrums when we are concerned with terms and sentences that concern physical events or actions depending on the structure of our body (since in every culture it either rains or it's a sunny day, and people eat, sleep, stumble or hop). But we have seen that one finds more difficulties in comparing the German *Sehnsucht* with an English equivalent, that *gemütlich* can be only imperfectly translated as *cosy*, and more vaguely as the Italian *accogliente*, and that even a common English expression such as *I love you* is used in contexts in which Italians would not use *ti amo*. We can say the same apropos concepts such as freedom, justice, friendship, dignity, God, death, crime and so on.

Semiotics, philosophy and cultural anthropology can discuss such discrepancies for years but a translator has continually to face them, here and now and every day. In doing so translators avoid ontological problems (unless they are translating a philosophical text): they simply compare languages and negotiate solutions that do not offend common sense (and if there are subtle connections between common sense and ontology, this is a subject for further philosophical debate). Translators simply behave like polyglots, because in some way they already know that in the target language a given thing is expressed so and so. They follow their instinct, as does every fluent bilingual person.

Thus, in order to stick to my purpose of not theorising too much, I would like to conclude by dealing with certain cases in which we do not speak of trees, ways of jumping, death, love or life, but rather of something that we are convinced we know very well: colours.

Colours

There is a text which had me puzzled for a long time. It's the discussion on colours that takes place in chapter 26 of the second book of *Noctes Acticae* by Aulus Gellius.[6] To deal with colours in the context of a text from the second century AD is a very difficult endeavour.

We are facing linguistic terms for colours, but we do not know to what chromatic effects these words refer. We know much about Roman sculpture and architecture, but very little about Roman painting. The colours we see today in Pompeii are not the colours the Pompeians saw; even if the pigments are the same, the chromatic responses are not. In the nineteenth century, Gladstone suggested that Greeks were unable to distinguish blue from yellow. Goetz and many others assumed that Latin-speakers did not distinguish blue from green. I have also found somewhere that Egyptians used blue in their paintings but had no linguistic term to designate it.

Gellius is reporting a conversation he had with Fronto, a poet and grammarian, and Favorinus, a philosopher. Favorinus remarked that eyes are able to isolate more colours than words can name. Red (*rufus*) and green (*viridis*), he said, have only two names but many species. *Rufus* is a name, but what a difference between the red of blood, the red of purple, the red of saffron, and the red of gold! They are all variants of red but, in order to define them, Latin can only make recourse to adjectives derived from the names of objects, thus calling the red of fire *flammeus*, the red of blood *sanguineus*, the red of saffron *croceus*, the red of gold *aureus*.

Greek has more names, Favorinus says, but Fronto replies that Latin, too, has many colour terms and that, in order to designate *russus* and *ruber* (red), one can also use *fulvus, flavus, rubidus, poeniceus, rutilus, luteus* and *spadix*, all definitions of red *aut acuentes eum quasi incendentes aut cum colore viridi miscentes aut nigro infuscantes aut virenti sensim albo illuminantes.*

Now if one looks at the whole history of Latin literature, one notices that Virgil and other authors associated *fulvus* not only with the lion's mane, with sand, wolves, gold and eagles, but also with jasper. *Flavae*, in Virgil, is the hair of the blonde Dido, as well as olive leaves; and the Tiber river, because of the yellow-grey mud polluting its waters, was commonly called *flavus*. The other terms all refer to various gradations of red, from pale rose to dark red: notice, for instance, that *luteus*, which Fronto defines as 'diluted red', is used to refer to egg-yolk by Pliny and to poppies by Catullus.

In order to add more precision, Fronto says that *fulvus* is a mixture of red and green, while *flavus* is a mixture of green, red and white. Fronto then quotes another example from Virgil (*Georgica*, iii, 82) where a horse (commonly interpreted by philologists as a dapple-grey horse) is *glaucus*. Now *glaucus* in Latin tradition stands for greenish, light green, blue-green and grey-blue; Virgil uses this adjective also for willow trees and for sea lettuce, as well as for waters. Fronto says that Virgil could also have used for the same purpose (his grey horse) *caeruleus*. This term is usually associated with the sea, skies, the eyes of Minerva, watermelons and cucumbers (Propertius), while Juvenal employs it to describe some sort of rye bread.

Things get no better with *viridis* (from which comes the Italian *verde*, green), since in Latin one can find *viridis* associated with grass, skies, parrots, sea, trees.

I have suggested that Latin did not clearly distinguish blue from green, but Favorinus gives us the impression that Latin-users did not even distinguish blue-green from red, since he quotes Ennius (*Annales*, xiv, 372–3), who describes the sea as *caeruleus* and marble as *flavus*. Favorinus agrees with this, since – he says – Fronto had previously described *flavus* as a mixture of green and white. But one should remember that, as a matter of fact, Fronto had said that *flavus* was green, white and red, and a few lines before he had classified *flavus* among various gradations of red!

Let me exclude any explanation in terms of colour-blindness. Too easy. Gellius and his friends were erudite; they were not describing their own perceptions, they were elaborating upon literary texts coming from different centuries. Can one say that they were considering cases of poetic invention where, by a provocative use of language, fresh and uncommon impressions are vividly depicted? If that were the case, we would expect from them more excitation, more marvel, and more appreciation for these stylistic *tours de force*. On the contrary, they propose all these cases as examples of ordinary language. Unable as they were to tell literature from daily life (or uninterested in daily life, that they only knew through literature) they proposed these cases as though they were examples of ordinary language.

The way of distinguishing, segmenting, organising colours varies from culture to culture. Even though some transcultural constants have been isolated, it seems rather difficult to translate colour terms from languages which are distant in terms of centuries or of space. If one uses the term *colour* to mean the pigmentation of substances in the environment, one has not said anything about chromatic perception: there is a difference between pigments as chromatic reality and our perceptual response as chromatic effect. The chromatic effect, it seems, depends on many factors: the nature of surfaces, light, contrast between objects, previous knowledge, and so on.

Daltonism represents a social enigma, difficult to solve, purely for linguistic reasons. To think that colour terms are simply denoting differences suggested by the visible spectrum is like thinking that genealogical relationships presuppose a unique kinship structure which is the same for every culture. Instead, in colours as in parenthood, terms are defined by their oppositions to and differences from other terms, and all of them are defined by a system. Daltonists have perceptive experiences different from those of normal people, but they refer to the same linguistic system.

Hence, the cultural facility of color blinds; functioning on differences in brightness – in a world that everyone else sees as differentiated by hue. Red-and-green color-blind people talk of reds and greens and all shades of it using the same words most of us assign to objects of a certain color. They think and talk and act in terms of 'object color' and 'color constancy' as do the rest of us. They call leaves green, roses red. Variations in saturation and brilliance of their yellow give them an amazing variety of impressions. While we learn to rely on differences of hue, their minds get trained in evaluating brilliance. Most of the red-and-green blind do not know of their defect and think we see things in the same shades they do. They have no reason for sensing any conflict. If there is an argument, they find us fussy, not *themselves* defective. They heard us call the leaves green and whatever shade leaves have for them they call green.[7]

Commenting on this passage, Marshall Sahlins[8] not only insists on the theory that colour is a cultural matter, but remarks that in every test of colour discrimination one assumes that classification of colours and utterance of colour names are linked to the representation of an actual experience. On the contrary, when one utters a colour term one is not directly pointing to a state of the world, but is rather connecting or correlating that term with a cultural unit, a concept due to a given segmentation of the chromatic continuum. The utterance of the term is determined, obviously, by a given sensation, but the transformation of the sensory stimuli into a precept is in some way determined by the semiotic relationship between the linguistic expression and the content culturally correlated to it.

To what sense experience does one refer to when uttering the name of a colour?

The Optical Society of America classifies between 7.5 and 10 million colours which can theoretically be discriminated. A trained artist can discriminate and name a great many hues, which the pigment industry supplies and designates with numbers. But the Farnsworth–Munsell test, which includes a hundred hues, demonstrates that the average discrimination rate is highly unsatisfactory. Not only do the majority of subjects have no linguistic means with which to categorise these hundred hues, but approximately sixty-eight per cent of the population (excluding colour defectives) make a total error score of between twenty and a hundred on the first test, which involves rearranging these hues on a continuous gradation scale. The largest collection of English colour names runs to over three thousand entries, but only eight of these commonly occur.

Thus average chromatic competence is better represented by the seven colours of the rainbow, with their corresponding wavelengths in millimicrons. This table could represent a sort of chromatic meta-language which guarantees the translation between natural languages, a sort of international jargon, according to which everybody could make clear to what portion of the chromatic spectrum they are referring.

800–650 Red
640–590 Orange
580–550 Yellow
540–490 Green
480–460 Blue
450–440 Indigo
430–390 Violet

Unfortunately such a metalanguage does not help us to understand what Gellius and his companions wanted to say. This segmentation corresponds to our common experience, but probably not to the experience of Latin-speakers. I think that Russian-speakers segment the range of wavelengths we call 'blue' into different portions, *goluboj* and *sinij*. Hindus consider red and orange a unified pertinent unit.

According to Conklin,[9] the Hanunóo of the Philippines have a peculiar opposition between a public restricted code and a more or less individual, elaborate one. They distinguish two levels of chromatic contrast. Let us disregard the second level, which seems to be a case of many elaborate codes differing between males and females and even between individuals.

The first level is represented by four unequal parts, mutually exclusive. The boundaries separating these categories cannot be set in absolute terms, and the focal points within the four parts correspond more or less, in our spectral terms, to black, white, orange-red and leaf-green. In general terms, *mabi:ru* includes the range usually covered for us by black, violet, indigo, blue, dark green, grey, and deep

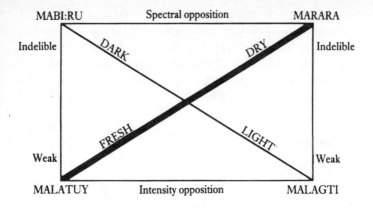

shades of other colours; *malagti* covers the spectral space of white and very light tints of other colours; *marara* corresponds to maroon, red, orange, yellow, and mixtures in which these tints predominate; *malatuy* is light green and mixtures of green, yellow, and light brown.

Clearly such a segmentation of the chromatic continuum depends on symbolic, i.e. cultural principles, as well as on the material needs of the Hanunóo community. First, there is an opposition between light and dark (*lagti* vs *biru*), then another one between dryness and wetness or freshness and succulence (*rara* vs *latuy*), which is relevant for plants (since most of them have succulent and often 'greenish' parts). Thus a shiny, wet, brown-coloured section of newly cut bamboo is *malatuy* and not *marara*. On the other hand, parts of dried-out or matured plants such as kinds of yellow bamboo are *marara*. A third opposition, which seems to divide the two aforementioned ones transversally, is that of deep, unfading, indelible substances, against pale, weak, faded, bleached substances, so that we see an opposition between on one side *malagti* and *malatuy* and on the other side *mabi:ru* and *marara*.

Let us now try to organise the Hanunóo system in order to make it comparable with our spectral one.

Such a reconstruction represents a complex system of oppositions and reciprocal borderlines. Geopolitically speaking, a national terri-

mµ	Average English	Hanunóo Level 1			
800–650	Red	Marara (dry)	Mabi:ru (light)	Mabi:ru & Marara (*Indelible*)	Malatuy & Malagti (*Weak*)
640–590	Orange				
580–550	Yellow	Malatuy (fresh)			
540–490	Green				
480–460	Blue	Mabi:ru (rotten)	Mabi:ru (dark)		
450–440	Indigo				
430–390	Violet				

tory is a negative concept: it is the class of all the points which are not included in the territory of the surrounding nations. In every system, whether geopolitical, chromatic or lexical, units are not defined in themselves but in terms of opposition and position in relation to other units. There can be no units without a system. The space of *malatuy* is determined by its – so to speak – northern boundaries with *marara*, and its southern boundaries with *mabi:ru*.

It is by considering this scheme (whose responsibility is mine and not Conklin's) that we can try to solve Aulus Gellius's puzzle. Let us simply complicate our previous diagram by inserting into it a hypothesis on the organisation of colours such as the one suggested by Gellius.

In this second diagram I consider not only the difference between different cultures, but also possible structural shifts within the same culture through the ages.

Rome, in the second century A D, was a very crowded crossroads of many cultures. The Empire controlled Europe from Spain to the Rhine, from England to North Africa and the Middle East. All these cultures, with their own chromatic sensitivities, were present in the Roman crucible. Gellius was trying to put together the codes of at least two centuries of Latin literature and, at the same time, of different non-Latin cultures. He must have been considering diverse and

mμ	Average English	Latin	Hanunóo Level 1				Hanunóo Level 2
800–650	Red	*Fulvus*	Marara (dry)	Mabi:ru (light)			～～～
640–590	Orange	*Flavus*			Mabi:ru & Marara (*Indelible*)		～～～
580–550	Yellow						～～～
540–490	Green		Malatuy (fresh)			Malatuy & Malagti (*Weak*)	～～～
480–460	Blue	*Glaucus*		Mabi:ru (dark)			～～～
450–440	Indigo		Mabi:ru (rotten)				～～～
430–390	Violet	*Caerullus*					～～～

possibly contrasting cultural segmentations of the chromatic field. This would explain the contradictions in his analysis and the chromatic uneasiness felt by the modern reader. His colour show is not a coherent one: we seem to be watching a flickering TV screen, with something wrong in the electronic circuits, where tints mix up and the same face shifts, in the space of a few seconds, from yellow to orange or green. Determined by cultural information Gellius could not trust his personal perceptions, if indeed he had any, and appears eager to see gold as red as fire, and saffron as yellow as the greenish shade of a blue horse.

We do not know, and we shall never know, how Gellius really perceived his *Umwelt*; unfortunately, our only evidence of what he saw and thought is what he said. I suspect that he was a prisoner of his cultural mish-mash.

Conclusions

This historical episode demonstrates that: (i) there are different segmentations of the spectral continuum; (ii) a universal language of colours does not exist; (iii) in spite of this it is not impossible to translate from one system to another; (iv) by comparing different ways of segmenting the continuum one can guess what the non-

European natives or our European ancestors meant by a given colour name; (v) to set up a table like this means to become able to speak many languages at a time; (vi) certainly, in order to elaborate on this table we have been obliged to choose a parameter, in this case the scientific division of the spectrum: in this sense we have shown a certain ethnocentrism – but we have done the only thing one can do when elaborating a translation manual, that is, to start from what we know in order to understand what we do not know as yet.[10]

If however we have more or less succeeded in understanding the Hanunóo system, we feel more perplexed apropos our conjectures about the 'poetic' segmentation or segmentations Gellius was thinking of. If we assume that the reconstruction of the Hanunóo system is correct, we would be able to use different Hanunóo terms to tell a fresh apricot from a dry one (even though in our language we would normally use the same colour term). With the terms of Latin poets, on the contrary, we have not tried to set up a system but have rather suggested that they established informal and imprecise sections of the spectrum.

In other words, the column of Latin poetry suggests that Latin poets (not necessarily as perceiving beings but certainly as poets) were less sensitive to clear-cut spectral oppositions or gradations, and more sensitive to light mixtures of spectrally distant hues. They were not interested in pigments but in perceptual effects due to the combined action of light, surfaces, the nature and purposes of objects. Thus a sword could be *fulva* as jasper was because the poet saw the red of the blood it might spill. Besides, we have seen in a previous chapter that Valéry saw the sea as having the silvery glare of a slate roof.

Gellius, decadent and synchretist, tends to interpret poetic creativity and invention as elements of a socially accepted code and is not interested in the relationship which colours had with other content oppositions in different cultural systems. But it seems evident that in every example in which Gellius quoted the poet, he tried to neutralise, so to speak, his everyday chromatic reactivity, in order to see and to show an unfamiliar universe of tints, in the sense of *das Fremde*, or of the *ostrannenija* effect advocated by Russian Formalists.

Those poetic discourses invited us to see the continuum of our experience as if it were never segmented, or as if our customary segmentation had to be radically changed. He was asking us to reconsider a horse, the sea or cucumbers in order to realise that perhaps they had no shades in common, irrespective of the chromatic province where our colour codes have situated them.

I think that a translator of these poets, in order to say what it means for a sword to be *fulva*, needs recourse, more than to a dictionary, to a table like my last figure. Only thus can one decide how to translate, in a given context, such terms as *rutilus*, *luteus* or *spadix*. If I look for *spadix* in a Latin dictionary, I'll find that it is a bay horse (that is, reddish-brown) but also that – botanically speaking – it is a frond torn from a palm tree. A dictionary is at most a starting-point. The real problem is to develop the ability to see the world as the poet saw it, and this will be the final effect of an interpretation of a text. After that, the choice of the right term can be either *target-oriented* (so that we shall translate 'reddish-brown') or *source-oriented* – and we shall choose *spandix*, to oblige our reader to feel *das Fremde*, which will oblige the reader to think of an archaic chromatic universe.

Once again, it will be a matter of negotiation between the translator, the reader and the original author, whose unique voice should remain in the text.

This is what I have tried to say, more or less, in the course of this book. Faithfulness is not a method which results in an acceptable translation. It is the decision to believe that translation is possible, it is our engagement in isolating what is for us the deep sense of a text, and it is the goodwill that prods us to negotiate the best solution for every line. Among the synonyms of *faithfulness* the word *exactitude* does not exist. Instead there is loyalty, devotion, allegiance, piety.

NOTES

1. Walther Benjamin, 'Die Aufgabe des Übersetzers', 1923, now in *Gesammelte Schriften* (Frankfurt: Suhrkamp, 1972). English tr., 'The

task of the translator', in Lawrence Venuti, ed., *The Translation Studies Reader* (London: Routledge, 2000), pp. 15–25.

2. Jacques Derrida, 'Des tours de Babel', in J. Graham, ed., *Differences in translation* (Ithaca: Cornell U.P., 1985), pp. 209–48.

3. *The Search for the Perfect Language* (Oxford: Blackwell, 1995).

4. Cf. Iván Guzmán de Rojas, *Problematica logico-lingüística de la communicación social en el pueblo Aymara*, mimeo, Con los auspicios del Centro internacional de la Investigaciónes para el desarrollo del Canada, s.d.

5. Eugene Nida, *Componential Analysis of Meaning. An Introduction to Semantic Structures* (The Hague/Paris: Mouton, 1975), p. 75.

6. I tried a first approach to this problem in *A Theory of Semiotics* (Bloomington: Indiana U.P., 1976), p. 80. Then I continued in my lecture 'Kleur als een semiotisch probleem', *Mondriaanlezing* lxxxi (1982), translated into English as 'How culture conditions the colours we see', in Marshall Blonsky, ed., *On Signs* (Baltimore: Johns Hopkins / Oxford: Blackwell, 1985).

7. Arthur Linksz, *Physiology of the Eye* (New York: Grune & Stratton, 1952), ii, 52.

8. Marshall Sahlins, 'Colors and Cultures', *Semiotica* xv/i (1975), pp. 1–22.

9. Harold C. Conklin, 'Hanunóo Color Categories', *Southern Journal of Anthropology* ii (1955), pp. 339–42.

10. It remains to ascertain if a Hanunóo speaker, starting from his own system, would be able to understand our own. Without making any hypothesis about the advantage of a given system, considered as more flexible than others, I suspect that a Hanunóo coming to Europe would behave similarly to a European Daltonist: he would adapt his sensations to our linguistic habits and would probably say *red* when Europeans say so.

Index

tr. in bold refers to a translation example.